LEADING
from Within

Other Books

Teaching with Fire, Sam M. Intrator and Megan Scribner, Editors

Stories of the Courage to Teach, Sam M. Intrator

Tuned In and Fired Up, Sam M. Intrator

Living the Questions, Sam M. Intrator

The Courage to Teach Guide for Reflection and Renewal,
Parker J. Palmer with Megan Scribner

JB JOSSEY-BASS

LEADING
from Within

POETRY THAT SUSTAINS THE COURAGE TO LEAD

Sam M. Intrator and Megan Scribner, Editors

FOREWORD BY MADELEINE K. ALBRIGHT
INTRODUCTION BY PARKER J. PALMER
AFTERWORD BY DAVID WHYTE

BICENTENNIAL
1807
⊛WILEY
2007
BICENTENNIAL

Published by Jossey-Bass
A Wiley Imprint
989 Market Street, San Francisco, CA 94103-1741   www.josseybass.com

Wiley Bicentennial logo: Richard J. Pacifico

Jossey-Bass books and products are available through most bookstores. To contact Jossey-Bass directly call our Customer Care Department within the U.S. at 800-956-7739, outside the U.S. at 317-572-3986, or fax 317-572-4002.

Jossey-Bass also publishes its books in a variety of electronic formats. Some content that appears in print may not be available in electronic books.

Credits begin on p. 249.

Library of Congress Cataloging-in-Publication Data

Leading from within : poetry that sustains the courage to lead / Sam M. Intrator and Megan Scribner, editors ; foreword by Madeleine K. Albright ; introduction by Parker J. Palmer ; afterword by David Whyte. – 1st ed.

    p. cm.

  ISBN 978-0-7879-8869-2 (cloth)

  1. Leadership—Poetry. 2. Poetry—Collections. I. Intrator, Sam M. II. Scribner, Megan.

  PN6110.L34L43 2007

  808.81'9–dc22   2007021352

Printed in the United States of America
FIRST EDITION
HB Printing   10 9 8 7 6 5

Contents

Defining Moments   29

Dare to Endure

Contents

Back At It   185

Foreword
by Madeleine K. Albright

One of the most moving stories to come out of September 11, 2001, involved a passenger on United Flight 93, which went down in Pennsylvania. The passenger, Tom Burnett, called his wife from the hijacked plane, realizing by then that two other planes had crashed into the World Trade Center.

"I know we're going to die," he said. "But some of us are going to do something about it." And because they did, many other lives were saved. Since that awful morning, the memory of their heroism has inspired us. It should also instruct us.

The reason is that when you think about it, "I know we're going to die," is a wholly unremarkable statement. Each of us could on any day say the same. It is Burnett's next words that were both matter-of-fact and electrifying. "Some of us are going to do something about it."

Those words convey the fundamental challenge put to us by life. We are all mortal. What divides us is the use we make of the time and opportunities we have.

Another way of thinking about the same question is to consider the recent discovery of similarities between the genetic code of a human being and that of a mouse. We are 95 percent the same. Perhaps each night we should ask ourselves what we have done to prove there is a difference. After all, mice eat and drink, groom themselves, chase each other's tails, and try to avoid danger. How does our idea of "have a nice day" depart from that?

It is possible, of course, that we are all so busy using time-saving devices that we don't have time to do anything meaningful. Or we may have the right intentions, but instead of acting, we decide to wait—until we are out of school, until we can afford a down payment on a home, until we can finance college for our own children, or until we can free up time in retirement. We keep waiting until we run out of "untils." Then it is too late. Our plane has crashed and we haven't done anything about it. We have lived our lives, but we have not led.

As the poems and commentaries in this volume attest, leadership is a concept with as many facets as life itself. The book's thesis, though, is that true leadership comes not from the sound of a commanding voice but from the nudging of an inner voice—from our own realization that the time has come to go beyond dreaming to doing.

The question of course is, What to do? The answer must be determined by each of us in accordance with our own circumstances and values, but the past has given us clues.

Leadership is found most often in simple acts of self-expression, when conscience overcomes reticence and we make our presence known by challenging a falsehood that has been advertised as truth, calling injustice by its name, stopping to help another, or on one memorable occasion, daring to take a seat at the front of a bus.

We think of great leaders as famous, and some of them are, inspiring others to follow: Gandhi kept on his desk a bronze casting of Abraham Lincoln's hand; Martin Luther King Jr. carried in his heart Gandhi's doctrine of creative nonviolence; generations of community activists have found their calling in response to the summons of Martin Luther King Jr.

There are, however, many more models created by people whose names will never be etched in marble or memorialized in a book. Leadership can be found in the reliable presence of a parent, the outstretched hand of a friend, the extra effort of a teacher, and the determination by any of us not only to ask the best of ourselves but also to encourage others to live lives rich in accomplishment and love.

Not every leader marches at the head of a band.

As America's secretary of state, I was privileged to represent my country in nations across the globe. I had many meetings with high officials in fancy offices, but these were not the meetings—or the leaders—I remember the most.

The people I will not forget are those I encountered in refugee camps and rehabilitation centers, in health clinics and safe havens for trafficked women and girls. These are the places where human character undergoes its toughest tests and where most people live on less money each day than many of us spend for a cup of coffee.

Among those I visited were women in Africa infected with HIV/AIDS. Because of the infection, they were shunned by their families. Other women refused to be tested to avoid being shunned, while many of the men refused to believe anything they were told about the disease or how it could be prevented. I held in my arms the children of such parents—children born with HIV and already dying from it. Some say the struggle against this disease is hopeless, but it is not.

For I also saw educators and health care workers fighting to stop the disease through truth-telling campaigns that were unafraid to shock. We know that such efforts make a difference, for they have already reduced infection rates and saved hundreds of thousands of lives.

While in office, I visited with children in Sierra Leone who had lost limbs in that country's bloody civil war. Some of the children were too young even to know what they were missing. I remember especially a little girl named Mamuna who wore a red jumper and who—while we talked—used her one arm to play with a toy car. Mamuna was three years old. I could not help but ask how anyone could have used a machete against that girl. After all, whom did she threaten? Whose enemy was she? Mamuna was not alone in the camp where we met. There were many others, of all ages, waiting for prosthetics to replace the limbs they had lost.

Yet, if there was self-pity in that camp, I did not see it. If there was anger and bitterness, I did not feel it. What I saw instead were teams of dedicated doctors and volunteers doing all they could to celebrate the gift of life.

I also visited poor neighborhoods and talked to families in impoverished regions from Haiti and Honduras to Burundi and Bangladesh. I saw people who lived a dozen to a room, or half a dozen to a cardboard box; people struggling to survive in crowded neighborhoods where nothing grows except the appetites of small children.

There are those among us who romanticize poverty; others just try not to think about it. But make no mistake, extreme poverty is a jail in which all too many of our fellow human beings are sentenced for life. Helping them to escape is not simple, but we have learned that progress can be made through a combination of giving more, teaching more, expecting more, empowering women, and developing more equitable rules for labor, investment, and trade. Above all, we need leaders who will not accept that misery and deprivation are inevitable, for failure to act to ease suffering is a choice, and what we have the ability to choose, we have the power to change.

We have learned that leadership on behalf of right can achieve miracles, or at least bring the impossible within reach.

Opportunities for leadership are all around us.

The capacity for leadership is deep within us.

Matching the two is this book's purpose—and all the world's hope.

A Note to Our Readers
by Sam M. Intrator
and Megan Scribner

This book brings together leaders from virtually every sector of society: corporate executives, surgeons, community activists, clergy, politicians, educators, lawyers, journalists, coaches, and more. These are tough and
tested men and women whose daily work life is chock full of problem solving,
relationship building, and make-or-break challenges.

Our invitation to these leaders was simple: take a moment away from the
sharp-elbowed context in which you do your work, step outside the cycle of
pressure and demand, put aside your role and title, and speak to us about who
you are, why you do what you do, and how you keep your heart and commitment alive in your work and leadership. In short, our interest was not in docu-
menting the latest process for organizational growth or in describing
techniques for optimizing effectiveness but in helping leaders tell the story of
what is authentic and genuine in their efforts to serve. To tell these stories—
stories of leading from within—we enlisted help in the form of poetry. We
asked each leader to reflect on a poem that mattered to him or her. These
reflections address what is personal and human in leadership. They offer snap-
shots of leaders encountering themselves and thus provide glimpses of the
complex geography of the leader's heart: what motivates, what inspires, what
hurts, what enthralls, and more.

We invited individuals to reflect on these questions because we believe that
the story of what animates people in their work and life is of great importance.

Work occupies so much of our life. It's not just that we spend vast amounts of our waking hours at work, but it is often through our vocational commitments that we engage the world. Our aspirations, our dreams, and even our understanding of who we are become shaped by the work we do in the world. And despite our efforts to keep perspective and to delineate between home and work and outside commitments, failure and success in the workplace reverberate throughout the circles of our life. In other words, work, as David Whyte tells us, is a serious matter. "It is where we can make ourselves; work is where we can break ourselves."[1] All of us, from those who lead great companies amid much fanfare to those whose leadership is less public, understand how high-stakes our work can be. When we care, we feel the bite of both success and failure deep in our bones.

Though so much of who we are is bound up in the work we do, the simple but crucial questions we asked—Why do you do what you do? How do you keep your heart and commitment alive?—often get lost in the giddyup world of our organizations and institutions. This book represents our efforts to listen to leaders make sense of their own stories and to share their passion, suffering, inspiration, and learning as they journey across the arc of vocation.

What makes our effort distinctive is our use of poetry to evoke stories of the work and leadership journey. Poetry by its nature can shake us up and turn us inward. Walt Whitman said that he wrote poetry because he wanted the reader to "stand by my side and look in the mirror with me."[2] Our project capitalizes on this reflective moment. It is a moment of disciplined stillness amidst the many demands of the life and work of leaders.

To fully appreciate this encounter that Whitman describes, we invited leaders to not only share a cherished poem but to write a 250-word commentary describing what happens when they reflect on the poem. We aspired to hear from a wide range of people—from those who identify themselves as conventional leaders to those who work quietly behind the scenes for worthy causes.

A Note to Our Readers

In our effort to secure a diverse range of voices, we scattered the call for submissions widely: we posted to electronic listservs, put up a Web site, wrote letters to leaders we admired, and beseeched friends and colleagues to invite those they respected to consider our invitation. In the end, we were gratified and overwhelmed to receive hundreds of responses.

As each submission crossed our desk or unscrolled on our e-mail screen, we felt as though we had been given the gift of bearing witness to a special and private communion between a leader and a poem. The commentaries are almost sacred in that they reveal a raw glimpse of an open heart striving to live and work with dignity and grace. An enduring image that stayed with us throughout this project and our prior work on *Teaching with Fire* is from Edward Hirsch's memorable book, *How to Read a Poem and Fall in Love with Poetry.* He describes poetry as a passionate, private communication from a soul to another soul. He also quotes the French poet Paul Celan, who believed poems were "messages in a bottle." We grew to love that image, in that we imagined ourselves standing on the shore uncorking these bottles and discovering not just the poem but the heartfelt response to it. We began to see our work as eavesdropping on a leader's meditation, and sometimes that took our breath away.

Despite the diversity of poems and contributors, the "bottles we opened" shared a fairly consistent message. Over and over, individuals told stories of a strong sense of purpose and the conviction to work for what they believed in. They were clear-eyed and matter-of-fact as they described the burdens of responsibility, the long hours, the high stakes, and the demands of decision making.

Implied throughout the submissions was a storyline on leadership that struck us as courageous. These leaders told us that leadership and work are journeys of uncountable obstacles and challenges. They described the enemy or the shadow side of leadership—those times when they feel vulnerable and ineffective and when they trudge through their days in a state of mindless reactivity. They named the human impulse to retreat and disconnect but articulated a conviction that the true test of leadership involves the courage to persevere and, in the face of failure and painful public criticism, to resist the temptation to become isolated. They knew that isolation from self, from others, and from animating beliefs is toxic to leadership and service.

Throughout the commentaries, we heard leaders say that meaningful leadership hinges on the leader being reflective, intentional, and self-aware. Leadership, they told us, begins from within. The task of effective, inspiring, and wise leadership (we heard) is for leaders to remain connected to their own values, principles, and beliefs—connected to colleagues, to the institutions they serve, and to the "best lights" and possibilities of their work.

All of us know the alternative. All of us have experienced leaders, colleagues, and professionals who treated us like widgets or chess pieces. The physician who touches your body but does not ask your name; the teacher who describes your child's struggles in school as if your son or daughter were a simple machine; the politician whose calculating positions have virtually no moral coherence; the CEO who renegotiates the unfathomably large salary, even while the company falters—and so on.

It would be an exaggeration to claim that reading, sharing, and talking about poetry can improve the bottom line or resolve nagging personnel issues within an organization. It's not commonsensical to assert that encounters with Keats or Neruda will translate into measurable outcomes or even result in leaders showing up the next day with amplified charisma, new ideas or strategies, or an idea for an innovative new product line. We'll leave that for other leadership books.

Poetry offers a different kind of vision. It traffics in imagery, metaphor, insight, energy, and emotion. In doing so, it speaks to the heart of matters crucial to leadership. William Butler Yeats could be talking about leadership when he says this about poetry: "It is blood, imagination, intellect running together. . . . It bids us touch and taste and hear and see the world, and shrink from all that is of the brain only." The leaders in this book get this. They see their work as of the heart, of the mind, of the spirit, and of the soul. Poetry, they tell us, is not ornamental to their leadership practice but indispensable because it provokes deliberation about living one's own truth and consideration of whether one's actions in the world are intentional, authentic, and congruent with the ancient Greek imperatives, "Know thyself" and "Become what you are." In other words, poetry provokes the reflection necessary for leadership from the inside out.

   As you traipse through this book and spend time with both the poems and the commentaries, it's worth keeping in mind the words of the great poet, teacher, and social critic John Ciardi, who writes:

> There is no poetry for the practical man. There is poetry only for
> the man who spends a certain amount of his time turning the
> practical wheel, because if he spends too much time at the
> mechanics of practicality, he'll become something less of a man
> or be eaten up by the frustrations that are stored in his irrational
> personality. An ulcer is the unkissed imagination taking its
> revenge for having been jilted. It's an unwritten poem, an
> undanced dance, an unpainted water color. It's a declaration from
> the mankind of a man that a clear spring of joy has not been
> tapped and that it must break through muddily on its own.[3]

While our organizations, corporations, schools, and other institutions strive for rationality, predictability, and efficiency, there must still be room for ways of knowing oneself, each other, and the world beyond the practical. Poetry, for all its precision, invites us to indulge that part of ourselves that deserves to become a "message in a bottle." Join us in uncorking these bottles and bearing witness to the depth and spirit of these inspired commentaries and poems.

Introduction
by Parker J. Palmer

The stories and poems in this book introduce you to nearly one hundred women and men who may change your understanding of what it means to be a leader. Some of their names are well-known, others not. But once you know their stories, you will recognize all of them as people of conviction, commitment, and everyday courage. And if you read this book reflectively, you may recognize yourself here as well—recognize yourself as a leader even if you are someone like me who has trouble embracing the role.

The truth is that we are all called to lead wherever we are planted: in the family, the workplace, the community. But many of us fear the challenges that come with leadership, and not without reason. If we could listen in on even the most effective leaders talking to themselves, we would hear a steady hum of stress and self-doubt: "What they're asking of me is impossible." "I'm damned if I do and damned if I don't." "I'm exhausted by the constant demands." "Someone else could do this better." Whether you are a mother or a magnate, it takes courage to lead and lead well.

Today, there is another obstacle that keeps some of us from embracing the leader's vocation: leadership itself has been given a bad name. We live at a sad, frightening, and maddening moment in American history, made so in part by the lack of integrity, compassion, and wisdom among some leaders. Who wants to say, "I am a leader," at a time when the word is too easily associated with pirates, prevaricators, and people with delusions of adequacy?

But as I learned more about the leaders in this book, I gained a new perspective on both the difficulties and disgraces of leadership. Because these leaders turn to poetry, not PowerPoints, for sustenance, inspiration, and guidance, they offer me real bread for the journey, not thin managerial soup. And because they are willing to wear their hearts on their sleeves—defying the myth that says leaders must appear invulnerable—I can trust them. By revealing their hearts and showing me how they get broken and yet made whole, these leaders help me take heart again.

Here are three brief scenarios to illustrate what I mean, each of them contrasting the heartfelt voices found in this book with the kind of "leadership" voice we too often hear in the land:

• A leader with the authority to send soldiers to their deaths speaks to the press saying, "Yes, many died today, but their deaths were altogether noble, the price we [sic] must pay for _____" (fill in the blank with a politically expedient and disingenuous phrase of your choice).

Compare that voice to the school superintendent who begins her contribution to this book: "It was the suicide that caused me to turn to this poem."—the suicide of a subordinate whose dilemma this leader had tried but failed to solve, compelling this leader to dig deep to find the courage to lead.

• A corporate executive at a meeting of stockholders tries to clothe acts of naked greed in a patently false "rational explanation" involving accounting protocols too esoteric for mortals to grasp.

Compare that voice to the founder of a successful ad agency whose contribution begins, "Leadership tries its little heart out to be rational. It is forever looking for . . . any logical way to . . . justify its position at the head of the table"—

and goes on to declare that, as important as true rationality is, caring for those we work with and serve is more important.

• A politician on the campaign trail gives a speech that panders to the basest bigotry of some voters, sometimes contradicting his or her true convictions in the process.

Compare that voice to a member of the U.S. House of Representatives who says, in her contribution, "As the first woman from Wisconsin and the first out lesbian in the nation elected to Congress, I am mindful of the role I play, both symbolically and substantively, in creating change."

I find the truth-telling in this book reassuring, bracing, and more: it encourages me to reach out, take risks, and put my hand to one of the countless close-at-hand leadership jobs that need doing. The leaders you will meet in the pages to come are among the many good people working away to rebuild the strong—yet fragile—communal infrastructure on which we all depend. They remind me that both you and I can join this reconstruction crew. In fact, we are probably already on it, perhaps wondering what we should do.

Emboldened by the stories found in the pages that follow, and as a way to honor their impact on me, I want to do a little truth-telling about my own struggle to embrace leadership and say a few words about the role poetry has played in helping me find my way.

Who's a Leader?

When I was in my thirties and forties, thinking of myself as a leader seemed not only uncouth but untrue. After graduate school, I worked for twenty years at a string of small, marginal institutions that, for all their merit, had little visibility and even less prestige. I did my work passably well. But I made no headlines, and no parades formed up behind me—though from time to time, imagining that I heard footsteps, I turned around to check. By the standards I held then, calling myself a leader would have been delusional, even more so than hearing those footsteps.

Now I am in my late sixties and things have changed. I write books that people buy, I am asked to travel and give speeches, and I have helped to create one organization and a few small projects that have touched the lives of a fair num-. ber of people. I am told that a small parade has formed behind my ideas but, thanks to good therapy, I do not hear seventy-six trombones, only a pennywhistle or two.

Still, I often resist thinking of myself as a leader. This resistance may come partly from the fact that I was raised by a father who regularly told me, "Just remember, Park, today's peacock is tomorrow's feather duster." And it surely comes from the fact that part of me is still in the grip of my youthful notion of a leader as someone who trails pomp, circumstance, and clouds of glory.

If those are the criteria of leadership, I have less claim to that mantle today than I did twenty years ago! In 1987, I left the last of those marginal institutions I worked for to become, well, marginal all by myself. I began working independently and for twenty years have had neither an institutional affiliation nor a bona fide job title. In their stead, I have a P.O. Box and a job description that is as hazy as they come: "writer, traveling teacher, and activist."

My office is about twenty feet from the bedroom, and I often work in my pajamas, robe, and slippers until after lunch. My closest colleagues are the UPS and FedEx drivers who bring packages to my door and doubtless believe that I am an invalid, under house arrest, or in the federal witness protection program. I have no assistant, secretary, agent, accountant, or lawyer, no newfangled personal Web site or old-fashioned business card.

My work life is so far beneath the radar that my own mother, during the last decade of her life, quizzed me again and again about how I was making a living or, more precisely, about whether I was making a living. My inability to say something concrete, like "I am the Associate Vice President of the National Association of Associations," left her with the dark suspicion that I was unemployed. To the day she died at age ninety-three, I think my mother feared that her only son—age sixty-something, pleasant enough and reasonably talented, but with no apparent means of support—might have to move into her basement on short notice.

This brief tour of my psyche may help you understand why the word *leader* has not always come naturally to me. Like many people, I reserved it for the special few. But at some point I had an insight that revealed how distorted my youthful standards for leadership were and how natural and widespread leadership actually is. Despite my occasional backsliding, this insight has helped me invest myself more deeply in my work and given me some critical questions to ask about my impact on the world.

The insight was simple: we are not autonomous individuals, some of whom are more Alpha than others. Yes, there are differences in social status among us, but they have more to do with perception than reality. And yes, those perceptions breed a version of "reality" that we have to cope with. But that version is only veneer. The deep and abiding reality—the reality we do not invent, the reality we really have to cope with—is that we are interconnected beings born in and for community.

If that is true, and surely it is, then leadership is everyone's vocation, and it is an evasion to claim that it is not. When we live in the close-knit ecosystem called community, everyone follows and everyone leads. Leadership, I now understand, simply comes with the territory called being human.

Everyone who draws breath "takes the lead" many times a day. We lead with actions that range from a smile to a frown; with words that range from blessing to curse; with decisions that range from faithful to fearful. Friends lead friends, parents their children, teachers their students, bosses their employees, doctors their patients, politicians their constituents. Of course, those roles and relationships often run in the other direction and can turn on a dime, as when constituents lead politicians, students teach their teachers, and young children provide wise guidance to their elders. And people can lead from the margins as well as from the center, which is the beauty part of any ecosystem.

My point is simple, though its implications are not: with every act of leadership, large and small, we help co-create the reality in which we live, from the microcosm of personal relationships to the macrocosm of war and peace. When I resist thinking of myself as a leader, it is neither because of modesty nor a clear-eyed look at the reality of my life. It is because I have an unconscious desire to avoid responsibility. That is magical thinking, of course. I am responsible for my impact on the world whether I acknowledge it or not.

So, what does it take to qualify as a leader? Being human and being here. As long as I am here, doing whatever I am doing, I am leading, for better or for worse. And, if I may say so, so are you.

Poets and Leaders

Our lives as leaders both demand and deserve reflection. They demand reflection because we must know what is in our hearts, lest our leadership do more harm than good. They deserve reflection because it is often challenging to sustain the heart to lead. It is here, within this force-field of demand-and-deserve, that leaders and poets can have creative encounters, as they do in this book.

Since it is more difficult to embrace what is demanded of us than what we think we deserve, let us turn first to the demand: as leaders, we all have an obligation to engage in self-reflection lest we lead unconsciously or mindlessly, heedless of our motives and blind to the potential consequences of our acts.

Socrates said that the unexamined life is not worth living. Now that I am old enough to amend Socrates instead of merely quoting him, I want to add one thing, for the record: if you decide to live an unexamined life, please do not take a job that involves other people.

The world has suffered deeply at the hands of leaders who possess the skill and the power to manipulate external reality but lack the foggiest idea of the inner dynamics that drive their actions. I once defined a leader this way:

> [A leader is] someone with the power to project either shadow or light onto some part of the world and onto the lives of the people who dwell there. A leader shapes the ethos in which others must live, an ethos as light-filled as heaven or as shadowy as hell. A good leader is intensely aware of the interplay of inner shadow and light, lest the act of leadership do more harm than good.
>
> I think, for example, of teachers who create the conditions under which young people must spend so many hours: some shine a light that allows new growth to flourish, while others cast a shadow under which seedlings die. I think of parents who generate similar effects in the lives of their families, or of clergy who do the same to entire congregations. I think of corporate CEOs whose daily decisions are driven by inner dynamics but who rarely reflect on those motives or even believe they are real.[1]

I believe those words name a critical truth about leadership. But it is a truth that is not well-served by the language of science, social science, or management theory. Inner truth is best conveyed by the language of the heart, of image and metaphor, of poetry, and it is best understood by people for whom poetry is a second language.

What is poetry if not, among other things, an instrument that helps us take readings of our own hearts? Here, for example, are the last three stanzas of William Stafford's "A Ritual to Read to Each Other." They challenge us to the core, but they do so in a way that gets the heart's attention, even when the intellect and ego want to resist:

And as elephants parade holding each elephant's tail,
but if one wanders the circus won't find the park,
I call it cruel and maybe the root of all cruelty
to know what occurs but not recognize the fact.

And so I appeal to a voice, to something shadowy,
a remote important region in all who talk:
though we could fool each other, we should consider—
lest the parade of our mutual life get lost in the dark.

For it is important that awake people be awake,
or a breaking line may discourage them back to sleep;
the signals we give—yes or no, or maybe—
should be clear; the darkness around us is deep.

First, there is Stafford's image of circus elephants on parade, each grasping with its trunk the tail of the one just ahead. Used to explore a weighty topic like leadership, it is an odd, funny, even ludicrous image. It reminds me of W. C. Fields's admonition, so pertinent to our times, that we must "take the bull by the tail and face the situation."

And yet those elephants can help us think afresh about the "ecological" understanding of leadership I suggested earlier—one rooted in the simple fact that we belong to a human community in which everyone follows and everyone leads. What is my impact on the ecosystem? is a decent question. But it is more abstract, less vivid, and therefore less challenging than the question, Where is this parade taking me, or where am I taking it?

If Stafford's image had been available to me as a young man, I might have seen that, even though I was not the commanding officer of a crack battalion or an elected official whose decisions affected millions, I was indeed lumbering along, trunk-in-tail, with a lot of other pachyderms and had been doing so for some time. Having seen that, and having had a good laugh about it, I might have been able to ask myself some important questions about where that parade was headed and where I wanted it to go.

In Stafford's poem, the elephants are headed for the circus. But the circus is not the poem's final destination—a fact worth noting in an era when some leaders still try to distract us from the world's darkness by offering bread and circuses; witness the way, in the wake of September 11, we were encouraged to fight terrorism by shopping. Stafford's poem takes us to the circus, but it does not leave us there. It uses the circus to ease us, even trick us, into a deeper and more challenging place than most of us want to go.

It is, indeed, cruel and "the root of all cruelty" to "know what occurs but not recognize the fact." Think about those moments when we refuse to know what we know—that someone close to us drinks too much, or that our personal lifestyle diminishes the life-chances of others, or that the corporation's accounting is as crooked as a corkscrew, or that war always breeds more war. To know such things and yet refuse to credit what we know, let alone act on it—that is surely a root cause of cruelty, one that leaders had best understand.

Then Stafford's poem takes another step, moving from diagnosis to prescription in the hope that we will come along. As only a poet can, Stafford appeals to "a remote important region in all who talk"—a region deeper than any polygraph can reach, a region that is inaccessible to mere rationality but that opens wide to the speech of the soul.

Stafford reminds us how easy it is, once we have fooled ourselves, to try to fool each other. Then he speaks prophetically about how dangerous life becomes when we do so, how the "parade of our mutual life" will most likely "get lost in the dark"—and he tells us what we must do if we want to find our way:

> . . . it is important that awake people be awake,
> or a breaking line may discourage them back to sleep;
> the signals we give—yes or no, or maybe—
> should be clear; the darkness around us is deep.

If we pachyderms-on-parade do not understand the meaning of that stanza in this disastrous opening decade of the twenty-first century, the darkness around us is even deeper than William Stafford imagined.

What Good Leaders Deserve

Too much leadership literature obsesses about the challenges of leadership, proposing tips, tricks, and techniques to make leaders more effective (hire a communications consultant) and their lives more bearable (take a vacation), while paying little or no attention to a sad but simple fact: much of the darkness around us comes from leaders themselves, who do things that make other people's lives unbearable. Leaders of every sort, in every walk of life, carry great responsibility. And our first responsibility is to do no harm. As the poet reminds us, the darkness around us is deep.

However, once a person has consciously embraced his or her leadership role and embarked on an inner journey to stay in touch with the soul's imperatives, life can and usually does get challenging. Many well-intended leaders have been done in by the foes of the good, the true, and the soulful: by institutions that seek survival over service; by the machinations of people who value personal privilege over the common good; by a stream of individualism that resists leadership of any sort; by the sheer grind of the leader's work, pushing boulders uphill only to find them rolling back down, sometimes atop the pusher.

These leaders understand Mark Twain's famous quip about being tarred and feathered and ridden out of town on a rail: "If it weren't for the honor and glory of the thing, I'd just as soon walk."

In the face of all the obstacles that confront conscious, caring leaders, it is good to know that poetry offers the comfort our souls deserve, as well as the challenges our leadership roles demand. Take, for example, "The Wild Geese" by Wendell Berry, a poem that offers authentic solace by reassuring hard-pressed leaders (who are often burdened by the scarcity assumption, convinced that they lack whatever it takes to get their jobs done) that they are surrounded by resources in abundance:

> Horseback on Sunday morning,
> harvest over, we taste persimmon
> and wild grape, sharp sweet
> of summer's end. In time's maze
> over fall fields, we name names
> that went west from here, names
> that rest on graves. We open
> a persimmon seed to find the tree
> that stands in promise,
> pale, in the seed's marrow.
> Geese appear high over us,
> pass, and the sky closes. Abandon,
> as in love or sleep, holds
> them to their way, clear
> in the ancient faith: what we need
> is here. And we pray, not
> for new earth or heaven, but to be
> quiet in heart, and in eye,
> clear. What we need is here.

What I love about this poem is not only its soothing pastoral imagery, its reminder that the madness of the human world can be countered by the sanity of nature, and its hopeful affirmation that "what we need is here." I love the fact that the poem does not ask us to take these truths on faith but invites us to discover them for ourselves by being "quiet in heart, and in eye, clear."

Quietude and clarity are both doorways into and destinations of an inner journey. They name what harried and hard-pressed leaders most need: not just the reassuring words of those who have found hope beyond the headlines but a path that can take us toward that hope in our own way, our own time, our own lives.

Poetry offers that path. In some mysterious way, poetry is that path. At a time when so many paths take leaders and followers toward deadly destinations, it is good to know about a path that can lead to life.

Note
1. Parker J. Palmer, *Let Your Life Speak*. San Francisco: Jossey-Bass, 2000 (pp. 78–79).

Called

The task of leading begins from within. It begins with a dream, a sense of what's possible, a commitment to a cause, a yearning to solve a problem, or a restless need to express one's creativity in service of the world. Vaclav Havel—the poet and playwright who lifted a movement for freedom with the audacity of his words and the steadiness of his heart—reminds us that the inward turn is not self-absorption but is critical to our effectiveness in the real world. In a speech to the U.S. Congress, Havel urged these leaders to take on the needs of the world, not through manipulation of external forces or political maneuvers but through engaging the human heart. "Salvation of this human world lies nowhere else than in the human heart—in the human power to reflect, in human meekness and human responsibility." Leadership begins from within. Power justly and humanely unleashed must work from the inside out.

The contributors in this section describe how they came to hear and understand their calling. We hear of mentors and role models who counsel, inspire, and provoke. The contributors describe "threads that are followed"; they speak of "jumping into work head first," of circuitous vocational journeys that, as one poet tells us, result in the "end of all our exploring/Will be to arrive where we started."

The theme of this section is the search for "work that is real" and the unrelenting effort to be self-conscious and attentive to one's own heart.

My parents loved poetry, and my ten brothers and sisters and I took turns memorizing poems for recitation at the dinner table. We favored the ballad poems. Tennyson, Kipling, and Robert Service were standard favorites. Most of my siblings can still flawlessly recite "The Cremation of Sam McGee," "Gunga Din," "The Charge of the Light Brigade," "Abdul Abulbul Amir," and "Casey at the Bat."

But my father's favorite poem and one we all memorized was Tennyson's "Ulysses." This is the story of Ulysses, in his dotage, rallying his friends for a last heroic journey. My father's last book, *To Seek a Newer World*, took its title from a line in the poem.

—*Robert F. Kennedy Jr.*

Robert F. Kennedy Jr. serves as senior attorney for the
Natural Resources Defense Council, chief prosecuting attorney for the
Hudson Riverkeeper, and president of Waterkeeper Alliance.
He was named one of *Time* magazine's Heroes for the Planet for
his success helping Riverkeeper lead the fight to restore the Hudson River.

Ulysses

It little profits that an idle king,
By this still hearth, among these barren crags,
Match'd with an aged wife, I mete and dole
Unequal laws unto a savage race,
That hoard, and sleep, and feed, and know not me.
I cannot rest from travel; I will drink
Life to the lees. All times I have enjoy'd
Greatly, have suffer'd greatly, both with those
That loved me, and alone; on shore, and when
Thro' scudding drifts the rainy Hyades
Vext the dim sea: I am become a name;
For always roaming with a hungry heart
Much have I seen and known,—cities of men
And manners, climates, councils, governments,
Myself not least, but honor'd of them all,—
And drunk delight of battle with my peers,
Far on the ringing plains of windy Troy.
I am a part of all that I have met;
Yet all experience is an arch wherethro'
Gleams that untravell'd world, whose margin fades
For ever and for ever when I move.
How dull it is to pause, to make an end,
To rust unburnish'd, not to shine in use!
As tho' to breathe were life. Life piled on life
Were all too little, and of one to me
Little remains; but every hour is saved

From that eternal silence, something more,
A bringer of new things; and vile it were
For some three suns to store and hoard myself,
And this gray spirit yearning in desire
To follow knowledge like a sinking star,
Beyond the utmost bound of human·thought.
  This is my son, mine own Telemachus,
To whom I leave the sceptre and the isle,—
Well-loved of me, discerning to fulfil
This labor, by slow prudence to make mild
A rugged people, and thro' soft degrees
Subdue them to the useful and the good.
Most blameless is he, centred in the sphere
Of common duties, decent not to fail
In offices of tenderness, and pay
Meet adoration to my household gods,
When I am gone. He works his work, I mine.
There lies the port; the vessel puffs her sail;
There gloom the dark, broad seas. My mariners,
Souls that have toil'd, and wrought, and thought with me,—
That ever with a frolic welcome took
The thunder and the sunshine, and opposed
Free hearts, free foreheads,—you and I are old;
Old age hath yet his honor and his toil.
Death closes all; but something ere the end,
Some work of noble note, may yet be done,
Not unbecoming men that strove with Gods.
The lights begin to twinkle from the rocks;
The long day wanes; the slow moon climbs; the deep

Moans round with many voices. Come, my friends.
'Tis not too late to seek a newer world.
Push off, and sitting well in order smite
The sounding furrows; for my purpose holds
To sail beyond the sunset, and the baths
Of all the western stars, until I die.
It may be that the gulfs will wash us down;
It may be we shall touch the Happy Isles,
And see the great Achilles, whom we knew.
Tho' much is taken, much abides; and tho'
We are not now that strength which in old days
Moved earth and heaven, that which we are, we are,—
One equal temper of heroic hearts,
Made weak by time and fate, but strong in will
To strive, to seek, to find, and not to yield.

—Alfred Lord Tennyson

I spent my summer teaching preschool and kindergarten in Tema, Ghana, through a program called Global Volunteers Organization. On the day that I arrived in Tema, my host mother brought me to the classroom where I would be teaching. After introducing me to the students, she indicated that I could begin to teach. I was jetlagged and hungry, but I dove in headfirst.

Education in Ghana is privatized; only children whose parents can afford the fees get to attend. Yet the quality of the education is still quite poor. The school I taught in was in desperate need of staff, and there were no teaching materials other than chalk and a blackboard. Still, I had to teach French, English, religion, art, math, and physical education. I found myself constantly running from one thing to the next. Lunches had to be cooked over an open fire and served, sick children had to be nursed, homework had to be written, issued, and corrected. Each day I struggled, feeling as though I wasn't making an impact.

Ultimately, I just had to get up each morning and offer the kids my best. This poem sustained me during that summer when I was feeling so doubtful. It sustains me still. When I become pessimistic about the situation in Ghana, I fall back on hope. I have to hope that there will be something better for these children eventually. I have to hope that things can change. I have to hope that my own talents can make a small difference.

—*Nicole Gagnon*

Nicole Gagnon is a senior at Smith College, majoring in education and child study and African studies. She has studied and taught in East and West Africa and plans to return to Africa for a career in disaster relief.

The journey to becoming a wise and effective leader begins with the work of understanding oneself. My journey began with a grandmother who scrubbed floors for a wealthy white family but had a vision that laid the groundwork for her grandson to have an Ivy League undergraduate and graduate education. She was so intrepid as to have a big dream (read: American) and to work hard enough to bring that dream to fruition for her children and their children.

As a black American, I feel an obligation to honor the fact that, despite our troubled racial history and the persistent presence of racism in too many aspects of our national life, the realization of my grandmother's dream happened here in America—nowhere else. This dream was buoyed through the generations by hope. I believe the ability of blacks to cling to a conception of what it means to be "American" that honors and celebrates our democratic principles while pushing to reconcile the enduring contradictions moves us ever closer to the ideal. As leaders we need to model, as best we can, what a life (professional and personal) lived with hope looks like. I love Alberta K.'s pride and the audacity that she has to appropriate the appellation "American" and boldly claim it as her own. Alberta K. embraces the difficulties of black folks' American past, because she knows it is the only way to seize the possibilities of our American future. I left Wall Street to become an educator because it strikes me that this is a worthwhile belief to share with our children.

—*Kyle Dodson*

Kyle Dodson is the principal of the Lee Academy Pilot School in Dorchester, Massachusetts. He was a member of the inaugural cohort of the Boston Principal Fellows Program, a one-year intensive program to train new leaders for the Boston Public Schools. Prior to his career in education, he was a mortgage-backed securities trader at PaineWebber, Inc.

Madam's Calling Card

I had some cards printed
The other day.
They cost me more
Than I wanted to pay.

I told the man
I wasn't no mint,
But I hankered to see
My name in print.

MADAM JOHNSON,
ALBERTA K.
He said, Your name looks good
Madam'd that way.

Shall I use Old English
Or a Roman letter?
I said, Use American.
American's better.

There's nothing foreign
To my pedigree:
Alberta K. Johnson—
American that's me.

—*Langston Hughes*

It's hard to say when it took root. It could have been when I was a kid tucked into a tent on our family's camping trips. Or it could have been its absence, growing up in New York City. In any case, my connection to the outdoors and nature had become an integral part of who I was before I left high school. By the time I graduated from college, I was leading mountaineering treks, sharing my passion for the natural world, and marveling at how it changed and humbled everyone.

In 1993, after months leading trips in the back country, I left the mountains. Ten hours later I was walking across the Lower East Side of Manhattan. The abrupt transformation of my surroundings crystallized my understanding that, although the wilderness seems endless when you are creeping up the side of a mountain with an eighty-five-pound pack on your back, the truth is that these places are small, fragile, and shrinking fast; saving them from our encroaching civilization is going to require a different kind of environmentalist.

Today, I am still following that thread through board rooms and trading floors in New York, Beijing, and Tokyo. I structure transactions that finance global greenhouse gas abatement projects. Environmental markets are a bare-knuckled way of keeping the cost of actions squarely in the calculus of investors, companies, and governments. Bumper stickers and recycling programs matter, but if we're serious about preserving this planet, we need to develop financial incentives for reducing pollution. "You don't ever let go of the thread."

—Michael Intrator

Michael Intrator is managing director of Natsource Asset Management, LLC, and responsible for trading environmental commodities, including EU Allowances and renewable energy. He executes transactions for certified emission reductions created by Clean Development Mechanism projects.

The Way It Is

There's a thread that you follow. It goes among
things that change. But it doesn't change.
People wonder about what you are pursuing.
You have to explain about the thread.
But it is hard for others to see.
While you hold it you can't get lost.
Tragedies happen; people get hurt
or die; and you suffer and get old.
Nothing you do can stop time's unfolding.
You don't ever let go of the thread.

—William Stafford

My shelves for years have held books my grandfather gave me—books about the Spanish Civil War (Orwell, Alvah, Bessie), about the Rosenbergs (he'd supported their defense and tried to help their orphaned sons), about religion (mostly against it), and philosophy (generally in favor but more Marx than Plato).

On a visit two years ago, when I asked how he was feeling, sitting almost immobile in a soft chair angled toward the window in his Florida sitting room, he talked about Milton's *Paradise Lost.* "In that book, the devil says a man's mind can make a heaven out of hell, or a hell out of heaven," he said. "So you ask me, how am I doing? In my body, I'm in hell, but with my mind, I'm trying to live in heaven."

The long poem by William Carlos Williams, "Asphodel, That Greeny Flower," includes these famous lines:

> It is difficult
> to get the news from poems
> > yet men die miserably every day
> > > for lack
> of what is found there.

I think my grandfather got that news and died with some notions of heaven—though he did not believe in heaven—in mind.

—Peter S. Temes

Peter S. Temes is founder and president of the ILO Institute, a think tank for corporations on the practice of innovation. He was president of the Great Books Foundation and the Antioch New England Graduate School. He teaches part-time at Columbia University and is the author of *The Just War* and *The Power of Purpose.*

From "Asphodel, That Greeny Flower"

Of asphodel, that greeny flower,
    like a buttercup
        upon its branching stem—
save that it's green and wooden—
    I come, my sweet,
        to sing to you.
We lived long together
    a life filled,
        if you will,
with flowers. So that
    I was cheered
        when I came first to know
that there were flowers also
    in hell. . . .
It is difficult
to get the news from poems
    yet men die miserably every day
        for lack
of what is found there.

—William Carlos Williams

I was the first in my family to go to college. On my first day, my mother held me in a warm embrace, looked me in the eye and said, "With this education you will be able to do anything you want to do. But be sure you are passionate about what you choose to do; do the work that is in your heart."

My quest to do work I loved and valued led me to create ChildrenFirst—a business providing parents with high-quality child care when their regular care arrangements were not available. I hoped, by holding a high standard for children's care, ChildrenFirst could be a vehicle for social change. In the work of nurturing and keeping children safe, good is not enough; only excellence should be accepted.

As ChildrenFirst expanded nationally, we served over fifty thousand children and two hundred corporations. The cornerstone of our success was our magnificent teachers. Heeding my mother's advice, we created a workplace where teachers could work in a way that "touched their soul." We wanted every teacher to be nurtured, honored, and developed to their fullest potential, not as employees but as human beings. In turn, our teachers were able to fully bring themselves to the children and families we served.

Just as my mother's hope, faith, and love enabled me to pursue the work of my heart, leaders must inspire others to feel a part of the mission of the work. It is then that we can accomplish what we cannot do alone.

—Rosemary Jordano Shore

Rosemary Jordano Shore is the founder and former chairman and CEO of ChildrenFirst Inc.—the nation's largest corporate backup child care company. She was selected as The American Women's Economic Development Corporation's 2003 Entrepreneur of the Year. Shore serves on the national board for the Center for Courage & Renewal.

How happy children are when we allow them to be creative—to laugh and to run freely as they wish. Do this and we are sure to see children who feel as if they are floating "on a cloud." This poem might well be a road map for floating. I sometimes wonder if I molded my career after the simple teachings of this poem.

As the head state coach for Massachusetts Youth Soccer, I help oversee 30,000 coaches working with over 200,000 children. My task is to teach coaches to see the game through the eyes of a child—each individual child. As coaches, we must realize and embrace the important role we have in children's lives. It is a role that carries much responsibility and transcends a simple game. We coach self-esteem, creativity, social skills, leadership, discipline, sportsmanship, coordination, and teamwork while promoting intrinsic motivation. As a teacher of coaches, I yearn for my coaches to personally connect with each child and find delight in the role.

In this poem, the piper turns himself into a singer and then to a writer. One could read this as being about limited attention spans or ephemeral taste; a second read suggests that Blake understood that we must always be experimenting with new ideas and playing with new methods as a teacher, a leader, and a coach. This poem reminds me to keep piping, singing, or writing, or doing whatever I need to do to make more children happy and to teach others to do the same.

—Michael Singleton

Michael Singleton is the head state coach and director of coaching for Massachusetts Youth Soccer. He also serves on the U.S. Youth Soccer's National Coaching Staff.

From *Songs of Innocence*

Introduction

Piping down the valleys wild,
    Piping songs of pleasant glee,
On a cloud I saw a child,
    And he laughing said to me:

"Pipe a song about a lamb!"
    So I piped with merry cheer.
"Piper, pipe that song again;"
    So I piped: he wept to hear.

"Drop thy pipe, thy happy pipe;
    Sing thy songs of happy cheer!"
So I sung the same again,
    While he wept with joy to hear.

"Piper, sit thee down and write
    In a book that all may read."
So he vanished from my sight;
    And I plucked a hollow reed,

And I made a rural pen,
    And I stained the water clear,
And I wrote my happy songs
    Every child may joy to hear.

                     —*William Blake*

I am the daughter of a country physician and nurse team. Growing up, the view from my front porch was of a large dairy farm and rolling meadows. This immediate and constant connection to nature and the ever-present life-and-death events in the home-based medical practice helped ground me in what really matters in life. My parents rejected materialism and commercial definitions of happiness. My father insisted on driving an old beat-up Ford, and my mother darned socks and taught us to put away food for the winter from our garden. At an early age, I came to understand the fragility and preciousness of life.

As my parents' daughter, I work with others to challenge the "more is always better" definition of the American dream. It's been an uphill struggle. Vehicles, houses, and malls have gotten bigger, while farmland, clean water, and human satisfaction have diminished. There is a connection between the slopes of these statistics. How do we pull away from excessive consumerism and reclaim more authentic sources of meaning?

Snyder's poem roots me in the answers to this question. We must stay connected to the flowers and unplug from technology. We need to reach across the ethnic and ideological barriers that divide us and stay together. And we must "go light."

There is a way forward, but it takes work. There are no advertisements that remind us to pick berries, have regular picnics in quiet places, or hang a clothesline. But this poem points the way.

—Betsy Taylor

Betsy Taylor is founder and board member of the Center for a New American Dream. She edited and coauthored *Sustainable Planet: Solutions for the Twenty-First Century* and authored *What Kids Really Want That Money Can't Buy.* She advises philanthropists and organizational leaders on strategies to promote a more equitable and sustainable society.

For the Children

The rising hills, the slopes,
of statistics
lie before us.
the steep climb
of everything, going up,
up, as we all
go down.

In the next century
or the one beyond that,
they say,
are valleys, pastures,
we can meet there in peace
if we make it.

To climb these coming crests
one word to you, to
you and your children:

stay together
learn the flowers
go light

          —Gary Snyder

When I left my first vocation as a college English teacher for a second as a pastor, my department chair pronounced on me a kind of ordination: "I guess you've worked in one form of higher education here, and now you're moving on to another. Here you're helping people not flunk out of school, and there you'll help them avoid flunking out of life."

I spent over twenty years as a pastor. I found the pastorate to be an ongoing conspiracy of resurrection. Roethke's beautiful poem came back to me often as I walked with people through the joys and struggles of life.

Now I find myself launching out on a third vocation—yet another form of higher education—as a writer-speaker-activist. Through books and conferences instead of sermons and services, I strive to bring the wrestling hope contained in Roethke's poem to people who—wounded, alienated, or disillusioned—are about to lose faith or have not yet found it.

For societies as for individuals, it is the struggle and strain of hope that brings about saintliness. Roethke's poem, linking the language-beyond-speech of spirit with the primal, wordless vigor of botany, encourages me to keep calling forth resurrection in everyone I teach and lead, always hoping against hope that they—and we—can rise. As a more vigorous hope rises in more of us, and as we come together in hopeful action, new possibilities can emerge between the "tight grains" of our world, and a better future can "put down feet."

—Brian D. McLaren

Brian D. McLaren (brianmclaren.net) served for twenty-four years as the founding pastor of an innovative church near Washington, D.C. Now he is an author and speaker and is on several boards, including Sojourners/Call to Renewal and Emergent Village. In 2005, *Time* magazine named McLaren as one of "The 25 Most Influential Evangelicals in America."

Cuttings

later

This urge, wrestle, resurrection of dry sticks,
Cut stems struggling to put down feet,
What saint strained so much,
Rose on such lopped limbs to a new life?

I can hear, underground, that sucking and
     sobbing,
In my veins, in my bones I feel it,—
The small waters seeping upward,
The tight grains parting at last.
When sprouts break out,
Slippery as fish,
I quail, lean to beginnings, sheath-wet.

—Theodore Roethke

What becomes of the hearts and spirits of children growing up in the midst of war and violence? How can I help? This has been my quest.

I started my journey in the Deheisha refugee camp in the occupied Palestinian territories. There I met five-year-old Nur, whose father had been killed when a bullet came through a window while the family ate dinner. I traveled to Mozambique and met Thomas, whose legs were blown off when he stepped on a landmine. I traveled to Nicaragua, Northern Ireland, Cambodia, and Angola, searching for answers. I learned that while children do suffer, many children marshal their resilience, fostered by caring adults, to become agents of healing and social change.

When I returned home, I was drawn to the Robert Taylor Homes housing project in Chicago, one of the largest, poorest, and most violent communities in the United States—a place where children are caught in the crossfire of gang shootouts and are not certain they will live to finish elementary school. Robert Taylor Homes—a place I feared—was a mile and a half from where I lived. But after exploring and learning on distant continents, I knew the children in this urban war zone had seeds of resilience that needed to be nurtured by caring adults.

The children—from distant lands and here at home—continue to teach me much about the human spirit—about love, forgiveness, and resilience—and what we can and must do to protect and nurture these precious resources.

—Kathleen Kostelny

Kathleen Kostelny is an international psychosocial consultant on children affected by war and violence. For two decades she has worked on behalf of children in war zones, including Afghanistan, East Timor, Sri Lanka, and Sierra Leone. She also works with children in the United States living with chronic community violence.

From *Little Gidding*

We shall not cease from exploration
And the end of all our exploring
Will be to arrive where we started
And know the place for the first time.

—*T. S. Eliot*

My father's highest accolade, the one that made our hearts sing, was, "You do good work." My parents modeled what it meant to "jump into the work head first"—through their approach to life which included their work as activists in Mississippi's civil rights movement.

The same spirit motivated my sister Christina, my best friend, my mirror image. Her passion for justice filled up the world. She died when she was thirty-three, and a friend fittingly read "To Be of Use" at her funeral. I have lived my life partly for her ever since.

The work still "has to be done, again and again" even more so after Hurricane Katrina brought into sharper relief the persistent problems of poverty and racial injustice. While exposing our unfinished business, it also generated a huge outpouring of offers of help. As president of the Mississippi Center for Justice (MCJ), I realized our job was to say yes to the offers from lawyers and law students who hungered to be of use.

Our historic precedent is Freedom Summer 1964, when a thousand volunteers came to support the heroic, homegrown movement that ended one hundred years of post-slavery apartheid. On the Gulf Coast today, with MCJ's help, dozens of lawyers and hundreds of law students are submerging in the tasks at hand, alongside the inspiring local leaders who picked themselves up out of the rubble of their homes and workplaces. Together, we are honoring our deep, collective desire to do good work and build a more equitable future.

—Martha Bergmark

Martha Bergmark has worked as a civil rights and antipoverty lawyer in Mississippi and as a national advocate for equal justice in Washington, D.C. She is president of the Mississippi Center for Justice, a nonprofit public interest law firm committed to advancing racial and economic justice.

To be of use

The people I love the best
jump into work head first
without dallying in the shallows
and swim off with sure strokes almost out of sight.
They seem to become natives of that element,
the black sleek heads of seals
bouncing like half-submerged balls.

I love people who harness themselves, an ox to a heavy cart,
who pull like water buffalo, with massive patience,
who strain in the mud and the muck to move things forward,
who do what has to be done, again and again.

I want to be with people who submerge
in the task, who go into the fields to harvest
and work in a row and pass the bags along,
who are not parlor generals and field deserters
but move in a common rhythm
when the food must come in or the fire be put out.

The work of the world is common as mud.
Botched, it smears the hands, crumbles to dust.
But the thing worth doing well done
has a shape that satisfies, clean and evident.
Greek amphoras for wine or oil,
Hopi vases that held corn, are put in museums
but you know they were made to be used.
The pitcher cries for water to carry
and a person for work that is real.

—Marge Piercy

On August 17, 1968, Senator Eugene McCarthy walked out of a Senate Foreign Relations Committee hearing after the undersecretary of state declared that Congress was "compelled" to support President Johnson's Vietnam policy. McCarthy was heard to say: "This is the wildest testimony I have ever heard. There is no limit to what he says the president can do. There is only one thing to do—take it to the country." And that is what he did.

I was twenty years old and joined thousands of Americans, young and old, marching from New Hampshire to Wisconsin, Indiana, Oregon, California, and New York, culminating in the Democratic National Convention in Chicago. It was six months of the purest experience of democratic grassroots politics-in-action that this country had ever seen and has not experienced since.

Eugene J. McCarthy was my uncle—my father's brother—a man who integrated poetry, philosophy, and political life. His thinking was complex, but his way was practical. In his poetry, his life, and his leadership, he called us to the responsibility of action—to offer our one and only life in service to what we love.

His call to action has influenced my life's work producing documentaries and films. Each film profiles the life and work of a remarkable person who knows that one person can make a difference and that when that person's vision is taken "to the country" it can inspire the lives of thousands.

—Mary Beth Yarrow

Mary Beth Yarrow has been producing documentaries and television films since 1979, including *The Willmar 8* (PBS/TV); *Intimate Portraits: Vanessa Redgrave, Liz Tilberis, and Bella Abzug* (Lifetime Channel); *Sidney Poitier "One Bright Light"* (American Masters Series for WNET-PBS/TV & BBC2); and *Sean O'Casey: Under a Coloured Cap* (RTE, BBC/Northern Ireland & BBC4).

Ares

god, Ares
is not dead.
he lives,
where blood and water mix
in tropic rains.
no, NNE, or S
or W, no compass—
only mad roosters
tail down on twisted vanes
point to the wind
of the falling sky
the helicopter wind
that blows straight down
flattening the elephant grass
to show small bodies crawling
at the roots, or dead
and larger ones
in the edged shade, to be counted
for the pentagon, and
for the New York Times.

ideologies can make a war
last long and go far
ideologies do not have boundaries
cannot be shown on maps
before and after

or even on a globe
as meridian, parallel
or papal line of demarcation.

what is the line between
Moslem and Jew
Christian and Infidel
Catholic and Huguenot
with St. Bartholomew waiting
on the calendar for his day
to come and go?
what map can choose between cropped
    heads
and hairy ones?
what globe affirm
"better dead than red"
"better red than dead"
ideologies do not bleed
they only blood the world.

mathematical wars go farther.
they run on ratios
of kill and over-kill
from one to x
and to infinity.
we are bigger, one to two

we are better, one to three
death is the measure
it's one of us to four
of them, or eight to two
depending on your
point of view.
12 to 3
means victory
12 to 5
forebodes defeat.
these ratios stand
sustained
by haruspex and IBM.
we can kill all you
three times
and you kill all of us
but once and a half—the game
is prisoner's base, and we
are fresh on you
with new technology.

we sleep well
but worry some. We know
that you would kill us twice
if you could, and not leave
that second death half done.
we are unsure

that even three times killed
you might not spring up whole.
snakes close again
and cats do, it is true
have nine lives. Why
not the same for you?
no one knows about third comings
we all wait for the second, which
may be by-passed
in the new arithmetic.
or which, when it comes
may look like a first
and be denied.

the best war, if war must be
is one for Helen
or for Aquitaine.
no computation stands
and all the programmed lights
flash
and burn slowly down to dark
when one man says
I will die
not twice, or three times over
but my one first life, and last
lay down for this my space
my place, my love.

—Eugene McCarthy

Defining Moments

The journey of leadership is marked by defining moments and crucible experiences. These events shape one's personal and professional trajectory. They are episodes that challenge us to find out who we are and what we stand for in our beliefs and values.

Leaders endure experiences where their courage and spirit are tested; leadership entails making conscious, high-stakes decisions when what is "right" is shrouded in gray. The poems in this section evoke stories that depict the discomfort and anguish leaders feel when they grapple with whether the daily work they do is congruent with their inner values. They describe those moments of core and sometimes uncomfortable deliberation.

In short, defining moments are those junctures in life and work where leaders are faced with an intentional choice—a time, as T. S. Eliot tells us, to wonder, "Do I dare? . . . Do I dare/Disturb the universe."

These moments, our contributors tell us, are a test of one's vision and imagination—moments that compel us to contend with what is possible and why. Amidst the uncertainty, leaders must act with courage and faith and be willing, as Naomi Shahib Nye describes, to "walk around feeling like a leaf./Know you can tumble at any second./*Then* decide what to do with your time."

Where does the moral conscience of the community lie, if it does not first lie within each of us? As Adrienne Rich makes dramatically clear, it is imperative that we become engaged in community. To be a sleepwalker and live only "a personal life" is simply not permitted.

The pull for me began with the tragic deaths of John F. Kennedy, Martin Luther King Jr., and Robert Kennedy. I was among the millions of Americans who were shaken and moved by those events and the troubling issues they raised. Those issues, then and now, are about equity, social justice, and race, but even more they are about the responsibility of the individual to stand up and be counted.

In the early sixties I became deeply involved in a small but serious community development effort in Roxbury, Boston's black community. The effort failed for many reasons but mostly because my well-meaning colleagues and I, all of us white, were rightly perceived as condescending and arrogant. It led to a memorable night when the vice president of the local NAACP became so angry that he threw a chair at us.

I learned the hard way that action without the participation of those involved is destined to fail. It's a lesson many of us still need to learn. How we talk to one another, how we listen, how we relate, may be the most important thing of all. If we do not get that right, our noble intentions will not work. It comes back to whether we choose to walk-through, or walk-in.

—Peter Karoff

Peter Karoff is founder and chairman of The Philanthropic Initiative (TPI). Prior to founding TPI, he worked for twenty-five years in the insurance and real estate businesses. A longtime board member for many nonprofits, he frequently speaks on philanthropic issues and is the author of *The World We Want: New Dimensions of Philanthropy and Social Action.*

In Those Years

In those years, people will say, we lost track
of the meaning of *we*, of *you*
we found ourselves
reduced to *I*
and the whole thing became
silly, ironic, terrible:
we were trying to live a personal life
and, yes, that was the only life
we could bear witness to

But the great dark birds of history screamed and plunged
into our personal weather
They were headed somewhere else but their beaks and pinions drove
along the shore, through the rags of fog
where we stood, saying *I*

—*Adrienne Rich*

The stakes were high. We couldn't afford to be bogged down in the usual stalemates and dissension. I persuaded a state environmental agency that we needed to do things differently. We needed the stakeholders—environmental activists and corporate entities—to come together and create the process and content for developing future waste policies.

The first gathering required a strong start to signal a change from business as usual. We secured a room at a local nature center and carefully prepared the agenda. As the facilitator, I knew it was my role to recognize the disparate but legitimate positions around the table but also set a tone that honored artistry and creativity. How we began mattered.

I had occasionally used poetry in settings readily receptive to that language; I'd never done so in this context. I knew dismissal would be deadly. I gulped and plunged ahead, reading Wendell Berry's "A Vision" at the start of the meeting. I called them to the power of the last two lines and how the "possibility" we had was in facing our "hardship" together.

There was a brief silence, and the atmosphere in the room shifted. There was "no paradisal dream"—this was hard work—but we ended up developing strong, innovative principles that all parties agreed to and that set a visionary tone for our work together.

Berry's last two lines serve to remind me that reaching for any dream requires risk and hard work; where we end up depends on where we begin.

—Barbara Hummel

Barbara Hummel has a consulting practice that focuses on leadership and collaboration within the corporate, government, and nonprofit sectors. She views her work as helping management and work teams begin the conversations they are wanting and needing to have.

A Vision

If we will have the wisdom to survive,
to stand like slow-growing trees
on a ruined place, renewing, enriching it,
if we will make our seasons welcome here,
asking not too much of earth or heaven,
then a long time after we are dead
the lives our lives prepare will live
here, their houses strongly placed
upon the valley sides, fields and gardens
rich in the windows. The river will run
clear, as we will never know it,
and over it, birdsong like a canopy.
On the levels of the hills will be
green meadows, stock bells in noon shade.
On the steeps where greed and ignorance
    cut down
the old forest, an old forest will stand,
its rich leaf-fall drifting on its roots.

The veins of forgotten springs will have
    opened.
Families will be singing in the fields.
In their voices they will hear a music
risen out of the ground. They will take
nothing from the ground they will not
    return,
whatever the grief at parting. Memory,
native to this valley, will spread over it
like a grove, and memory will grow
into legend, legend into song, song
into sacrament. The abundance of this
    place,
the songs of its people and its birds,
will be health and wisdom and indwelling
light. This is no paradisal dream.
Its hardship is its possibility.

—Wendell Berry

When I first came to work at the Sierra Club, I was given the task of coordinating the media work of over a hundred grassroots organizers around the country, many of whom had been working in the field for decades and were not always receptive to the ideas of an inexperienced and energetic twenty-four-year-old. How was I, only one year out of college, supposed to effectively train people who were taken aback by my youth?

It took time for me to earn the respect of my colleagues, and in time I learned that training is as much about listening as it is about teaching.

I love this poem because it reminds me that all leaders, artists, and innovators have moments of great doubt. Even William Shakespeare was no exception. Tucked away in "Sonnet 29" is a remarkable line where he bemoans his fate, wishing he had "this man's art, or that man's scope." Shakespeare's confession to feelings of inadequacy offers me solace and strength.

I have a note stuck to my computer listing the three qualities that a Zen master once taught are necessary for progress: great faith, great doubt, and great effort. I try to remember that when I am feeling discouraged. Doubt is a natural part of my work, sometimes even a helpful one, because it forces me to re-evaluate my positions.

Luckily for us, Shakespeare did not let his doubts paralyze him. He worked through them—and gave us true, deep, lasting art as a result.

—*Orli Cotel*

Orli Cotel is the national publicist for the Sierra Club, the country's oldest and largest grassroots environmental group. She also directs the Sierra Club's media training program, helping organizers learn strategic media skills. As a grassroots organizer, Orli has worked with volunteers on conservation campaigns in New Orleans, Tahoe, Cleveland, and Philadelphia.

Sonnet 29

When, in disgrace with fortune and men's eyes,
I all alone beweep my outcast state
And trouble deaf heaven with my bootless cries,
And look upon myself and curse my fate,
Wishing me like to one more rich in hope,
Featur'd like him, like him with friends possess'd,
Desiring this man's art, and that man's scope,
With what I most enjoy contented least;
Yet in these thoughts myself almost despising,
Haply I think on thee, and then my state,
Like to the lark at break of day arising
From sullen earth, sings hymns at heaven's gate;
    For thy sweet love rememb'red such wealth brings
    That then I scorn to change my state with kings.

—William Shakespeare

Years ago, when I was a seminary student, I taught swimming lessons at the local Y to four- and five-year-olds. It was a remarkable experience, for it was there that I learned something profound about the meaning of faith and the nature of God's grace.

Every Saturday morning, eight or nine little children descended from the locker rooms, clutching their towels, ready to face deep waters. They needed my help, but week by week, as I held each one in my arms and carried them out away from the hard, safe surface of the deck of the pool, they gradually learned to trust a force they could neither see nor understand. In order to swim, they needed to learn, in a way no physics lesson could ever teach them, the buoyancy of water. They needed to come to know, in their bodies and in their hearts, that the water itself can hold them up, if only they can relax their limbs, breathe deeply and slowly, and rest upon it.

So it is with the life of faith. Faith, like swimming, requires a specific kind of knowledge—profoundly personal and existential but still quite objective nonetheless. Faith is the knowledge of the reality of God's buoyancy—of God's upholding love and mercy, present to the world and to us all in every situation and circumstance of life. Faith is life lived resting on God's grace. When I finally learned that, my life changed for good. This poem is my prayer.

—*Craig Dykstra*

Craig Dykstra is a Presbyterian minister; for eighteen years, he has served as vice president for religion at the Lilly Endowment, a private charitable foundation. He previously served on the faculties of Princeton Theological Seminary and Louisville Presbyterian Theological Seminary and was a pastor at the Westminster Presbyterian Church of Detroit.

The Avowal

As swimmers dare
to lie face to the sky
and water bears them,
as hawks rest upon air
and air sustains them,
so would I learn to attain
freefall, and float
into Creator Spirit's deep embrace,
knowing no effort earns
that all-surrounding grace.

—Denise Levertov

A key moment in all leaders' tenure comes the first time they publicly stand before those they have been entrusted to serve and lead. My inauguration as president of Southwestern University (where I still serve) was my moment.

I worked hard on my remarks, hoping to convey my vision for the university but also to share who I was and how my journey, which began in Sugar Land, Texas, and meandered through Georgia, Connecticut, and Pennsylvania, had brought me home to Southwestern, where thirty-eight years before I had served as student government president.

I decided to close by reciting "The seven of pentacles" because it speaks to me of the struggle to find congruity between vocational calling and living a life that matters and is loving—what I value as a leader and a person. I hoped to convey these principles to those gathered:

- That which is worth cultivating takes time.
- We must be diligent about taking care of what is important, what is lasting.
- We cannot always see or understand how things or ideas grow and manifest themselves. Sometimes this happens quietly, without fanfare.
- We should strive to make connections so that we catch a glimpse of the interdependence of life, lives, and ideas.
- We should live a life of integrity so that we can love ourselves and others.
- If we like the way we have chosen to live, we live a life rich with meaning and, just maybe, experience genuine joy. This is the harvest.

—Jake B. Schrum

Jake B. Schrum is president of Southwestern University and has been a college administrator for thirty-three years. He is most interested in the way people treat each other in the workplace. He receives great joy from mentoring young administrators.

The seven of pentacles

Under a sky the color of pea soup
she is looking at her work growing away there
actively, thickly like grapevines or pole beans
as things grow in the real world, slowly enough.
If you tend them properly, if you mulch, if you water,
if you provide birds that eat insects a home and winter food,
if the sun shines and you pick off caterpillars,
if the praying mantis comes and the ladybugs and the bees,
then the plants flourish, but at their own internal clock.

Connections are made slowly, sometimes they grow underground.
You cannot tell always by looking what is happening.
More than half a tree is spread out in the soil under your feet.
Penetrate quietly as the earthworm that blows no trumpet.
Fight persistently as the creeper that brings down the tree.
Spread like the squash plant that overruns the garden.
Gnaw in the dark and use the sun to make sugar.

Weave real connections, create real nodes, build real houses.
Live a life you can endure: make love that is loving.
Keep tangling and interweaving and taking more in,
a thicket and bramble wilderness to the outside but to us
interconnected with rabbit runs and burrows and lairs.

Live as if you liked yourself, and it may happen:
reach out, keep reaching out, keep bringing in.
This is how we are going to live for a long time: not always,
for every gardener knows that after the digging, after the planting,
after the long season of tending and growth, the harvest comes.

—*Marge Piercy*

"No" is not a word that I speak easily. How can I take time for myself when there are so many in need? How can I learn to say "No" so that my "Yes" has real meaning? Naomi Shihab Nye's poem teases through the layers of social obligation with which I so often clothe myself.

As a rabbi and a psychotherapist, I do my work with my community based in Seattle and the mini-communities wherever I teach. I do my work in my relationships and in my counseling. But there are endless piles of paper demanding my attention, e-mails piling up in my in-box, and telephone messages stacking up on my desk. There is so much that conspires to pull me away from what I really want to do with my time. Sometimes it seems a miracle I've had time for my own spiritual work.

Yet with all this, I am actually able to do what I love to do. Two of my best friends are the Christian pastor and the Muslim minister with whom I do a weekly interfaith talk radio program. After an interfaith service that we convened together after 9/11, we maintained our commitment to work together and have co-led an interfaith spiritual journey to Israel. We are now writing a book on interfaith spirituality. Interfaith is not just public work; it is private as well. My greatest challenge is to remember what is really important. It is fitting that I am called to my remembering by the words of a Palestinian-American poet.

—Ted Falcon

Ted Falcon, a rabbi and pioneer in reclaiming and expanding ancient Jewish spiritual teachings, founded two meditative synagogues—Makom Ohr Shalom in Los Angeles and Bet Alef Meditative Synagogue in Seattle. He celebrates a spirituality that supports personal and community healing and naturally expresses as more compassionate action in the world.

The Art of Disappearing

When they say Don't I know you?
say no.

When they invite you to the party
remember what parties are like
before answering.
Someone telling you in a loud voice
they once wrote a poem.
Greasy sausage balls on a paper plate.
Then reply.

If they say We should get together
say why?

It's not that you don't love them anymore.
You're trying to remember something
too important to forget.

Trees. The monastery bell at twilight.
Tell them you have a new project.
It will never be finished.

When someone recognizes you in a grocery
  store
nod briefly and become a cabbage.
When someone you haven't seen in ten
  years
appears at the door,
don't start singing him all your new songs.
You will never catch up.

Walk around feeling like a leaf.
Know you could tumble any second.
·Then decide what to do with your time.

—*Naomi Shihab Nye*

Decision making is integral to leadership. As a college president, I lead the decision making on a range of issues: visionary, financial, academic, and administrative. While decision making is one of the most daunting aspects of my work, I am reassured by Eliot's sense that decisions are made within the context of a moment. He invites us to bring ourselves to the current moment, interpret it carefully, and respond to it passionately. He encourages us to be decisive, even though our decisions may not survive the next moment. I find his insight profoundly liberating.

Eliot instructs us that we have the capacity to do or undo, begin or end, and maintain or change. Some leaders seem to think that reversing or even changing directions is a sign of weakness—I find it a sign of strong leadership.

Academic programs thrive on student interest. A well-designed program may be ahead of market trends and need to be put on hold. Despite the ensuing disappointment, I have at times decided to delay such a program until student interest catches up with the proposal. Then I'm able to reverse my decision and give the go-ahead.

Each time I return to this poem, I am reminded not to worry about time running out or to fear that what I have accomplished may end up in a bureaucratic junk heap. Even while accepting that my decisions can be revised and even reversed by my successors, my enduring satisfaction as a leader lies in serving my moment well.

—Joseph L. Subbiondo

Joseph L. Subbiondo is president of the California Institute of Integral Studies. He has also been the dean of the College of Arts and Sciences at Santa Clara University and the liberal arts dean at Saint Mary's College of California. His field of scholarly inquiry is the history of linguistics.

From "The Love Song of J. Alfred Prufrock"

And indeed there will be time
For the yellow smoke that slides along the street,
Rubbing its back upon the window-panes;
There will be time, there will be time
To prepare a face to meet the faces that you meet;
There will be time to murder and create,
And time for all the works and days of hands
That lift and drop a question on your plate;
Time for you and time for me,
And time yet for a hundred indecisions,
And for a hundred visions and revisions,
Before the taking of a toast and tea. . . .

And indeed there will be time
To wonder, "Do I dare?" and, "Do I dare?". . .
Do I dare
Disturb the universe?
In a minute there is time
For decisions and revisions which a minute will reverse.

—T. S. Eliot

William Ayot's leader's courageous heart pulses with an essential, consistent, persistent purpose. Behind the leader's words and actions I see inner strength. I yearn for a leader like this! I could dedicate myself to a leader like this!

Midpoem I look up and see myself slipping toward a worshipful follower role: you lead; you know better. I'm tired of being responsible, tired of meeting others' expectations. You lead; you stand on the deck when the wave hits the rock. I'll stand over here and watch. As I read the poem; I sense a part of me stepping aside, not measuring up to my ideals, my potential. And, at the same time, another small voice in me says, I want to be that leader. I want to be that courageous leader I yearn for. Yet I don't know all the currents; I can't hold all the doubts; I can't bear all the hopes and expectations.

I see my personal dynamic playing out across organizations, across our country. We idealize and idolize heroic leaders and when we compare ourselves to those leaders, we find ourselves lacking. When others offer themselves as leaders, we ask them to speak heroic words; we embrace them as they speak to our need for the perfect leader. Later, when they invariably fail to live up to our ideals, we cast them aside and continue our search for our idealized, heroic, and impossible leader. Leadership must honor, even celebrate, the reality of our very human dimensions if you and I are to lead.

—*Geoff Bellman*

Geoff Bellman has been leading and consulting to leaders for forty years. He's the author of five books on organizations, change, life, and work, including *Getting Things Done When You Are Not in Charge* and *The Beauty of the Beast: Breathing New Life into Organizations.*

The Contract

A word from the led

And in the end we follow them—
not because we are paid,
not because we might see some advantage,
not because of the things they have accomplished,
not even because of the dreams they dream
but simply because of who they are:
the man, the woman, the leader, the boss
standing up there when the wave hits the rock,
passing out faith and confidence like life jackets,
knowing the currents, holding the doubts,
imagining the delights and terrors of every landfall:
captain, pirate, and parent by turns,
the bearer of our countless hopes and expectations.
We give them our trust. We give them our effort.
What we ask in return is that they stay true.

—*William Ayot*

After decades of yearning, I finally earned my pilot's license. My motivation was neither acrobatic thrills (I hate roller coasters) nor a midlife crisis (as I said, I hate roller coasters). No, my desire grew out of what writer Selden Rodman has called the poetry of flight.

Anyone who's ever glanced out an airplane window has beheld cumulus cloud sculptures and painted landscapes passing below. Flight is as much about aesthetics as it is about aeronautics.

Perhaps this is why more than a few pilots have been writers and artists. Leonardo da Vinci sketched flying machines, even as he painted the Mona Lisa. Antoine de Saint-Exupéry was one of the world's first airmail pilots before he wrote *Le Petit Prince*.

The art of leadership and the poetry of flight are not as disparate as they seem. As a preacher I have learned that elevating Word and Sacrament requires the gravity-defying courage of a poet. As a leader of a new nonprofit, I could only explain our path-breaking work by means of the metaphor that we were "building the airplane while flying it." I have discovered that if the organizations I lead are to soar, I must be a poet of flight.

Flying has thus taught me the poetry of leading with courage. Like two generations of pilots and leaders alike, I have been inspired by Amelia Earhart's "Courage." It is no surprise that her first poems were submitted for publication the same year she became a pilot.

—John Wimmer

John Wimmer is a program director at the Lilly Endowment Inc., with responsibility for grant making in theological education, pastoral leadership development, and congregational life. Previously, he was a local pastor, professor, and administrator at a church-related college, and founding president of the Indianapolis Center for Congregations. He flies a Cessna Skyhawk.

Courage

Courage is the price which life exacts for granting peace.
The soul that knows it not, knows no release
From little things;

Knows not the livid loneliness of fear
nor mountain heights, where bitter joy can hear
The sound of wings.

How can life grant us boon of living, compensate
For dull gray ugliness and pregnant hate
Unless we dare

The soul's dominion? Each time we make a choice we pay
With courage to behold resistless day
And count it fair.

—Amelia Earhart

When I think of the people who have meant the most to me in my life, they haven't been leaders in the conventional sense. Rather they've been like the father in William Stafford's poem—people who listen for what they can hear, far off in the night, "from that other place." They hear so much that they make me want to listen, too.

How can I listen so that others can hear things they have never heard before and say things they have never thought to say? That's my goal as a freelance journalist. I don't want the people I'm interviewing to repeat the same words they've said a thousand times before. I want them to share something from a deeper place that is original yet so true that it has meaning for us all.

During the first interview I ever did, I learned that this is possible. It was with the Norwegian actress Liv Ullmann. Throughout the interview, she absorbed my questions and listened for what she would say with the inner focus and intensity that she's known for in her performances. It made me listen all the more as we talked. Working together in this fashion allowed something fresh and profound to emerge. She wove together her insights on acting and her deepest thoughts on life and what it means to be truly human in a way that I've never seen anyone do before or since.

That day I learned that listening is wonderfully contagious.

—*David Brooks Andrews*

David Brooks Andrews has worked as a writer for thirty years. For the last ten years, he has covered theater and the arts for the *MetroWest Daily News* and the *Standard-Times* in Massachusetts. He also works as a freelance photographer.

Listening

My father could hear a little animal step,
or a moth in the dark against the screen,
and every far sound called the listening out
into places where the rest of us had never been.

More spoke to him from the soft wild night
than came to our porch for us on the wind;
we would watch him look up and his face go keen
till the walls of the world flared, widened.

My father heard so much that we still stand
inviting the quiet by turning the face,
waiting for a time when something in the night
will touch us too from that other place.

—*William Stafford*

Transitions begin with endings. As I prepared to leave an organization I founded and led for nineteen years, the prospect of leaving the people and the work I loved filled me with unease and sadness. The transition proved to be harder than I expected. Over my last year, I experienced a great sense of grief, even as I anticipated exciting new work. During that time, I received outpourings of praise, appreciation, and affection, even as I experienced the inevitable pulling away that is a natural part of leave-taking. Toward the end of my tenure, my emotions were very close to the surface, and a smile from a colleague or a "How are you?" from almost anyone could, embarrassingly, bring on tears.

A dear colleague shared this poem with me, and I found it both instructive and comforting. Being a leader requires the capacity for letting go—letting go of a long-held identity, letting go of the images other people have of you, and letting go of one's attachment to particular ideas or ways of working. As I journeyed through this transition, my biggest challenge was to let go of my desire to leave the organization in a perfect state for its next leader, with no loose ends and everything wrapped up in a neat package. This poem helped me to play with saying goodbye. I practiced letting it roll off my tongue and found myself whispering softly, "adios." Now I can sing it as I honor where I've been and where I'm going.

—*Pamela Seigle*

Pamela Seigle is executive director of Courage & Renewal Northeast. She founded and served for nineteen years as the executive director of the Open Circle Social Competency Program—a nationally recognized social and emotional learning program for elementary schools.

Adios

It is a good word, rolling off the tongue
no matter what language you were born with.
Use it. Learn where it begins,
the small alphabet of departure,
how long it takes to think of it,
then say it, then be heard.

Marry it. More than any golden ring
it shines, it shines.
Wear it on every finger
till your hands dance,
touching everything easily,
letting everything, easily, go.

Strap it to your back like wings.
Or a kite-tail. The stream of air behind a jet.
If you are known for anything,
let it be the way you rise out of sight
when your work is finished.

Think of things that linger: leaves,
cartons and napkins, the damp smell
    of mold.

Think of things that disappear.

Think of what you love best,
what brings tears into your eyes.

Something that said *adios* to you
before you knew what it meant
or how long it was for.

Explain little, the word explains itself.
Later perhaps. Lessons following lessons,
like silence following sound.

—*Naomi Shihab Nye*

Sometimes It Aches

$\mathcal{L}$ angston Hughes tells us, "Well, son, I'll tell you:/Life for me ain't been no crystal stair./It's had tacks in it, and splinters." So it is with every leader's journey, despite our culture's yearning to see those in charge as unruffled and implacable.

Judy Brown's poem describes the inevitable in every leader's journey: "There is a trough in waves, a low spot." In that trough, amidst the tacks and splinters, there can be, as David Whyte tells us, "unspeakable pain."

These poems and stories of leadership describe the anguish and uncertainty of the trough. We hear of "being lost" and journeys interrupted by "deep holes in one's being." We hear of suffering endured in public and the ache of keeping your chin up when your heart is breaking open.

These leaders describe what it means to lead while being wounded. They describe the bone-aching weariness of fighting for a good cause and how it is that they keep on going. They tell of how somewhere in their lives they can hear a mentor, like the one in Hughes's poem, who reminds them, "Don't you turn back./Don't you step down on the steps./Don't you fall now—/For I'se still goin', honey."

It was the suicide that caused me to turn to this poem. As a school administrator for nineteen years, I had finally become the superintendent, with responsibility for twenty-three school districts, each with its own board of education and superintendent. Within months of my appointment, a fierce struggle erupted between the board and the superintendent-principal of one of the smallest districts. No skill, insight, or power I possessed could bring resolution to the turmoil. Lawyers, bureaucracies, and politicians intervened, but the battle escalated.

It was Sunday night. I returned home to an answering machine with flashing lights. I pushed "mailbox one" to hear that the superintendent, a forty-three-year-old woman, had committed suicide.

Subsequent messages were death threats, reporters' questions, and angry voices calling me "murderer." My world spun out. The next morning, a team and I went into the district. The following day we sat in the auditorium with five-year-olds who wanted to know why she was gone and what suicide was. At night, the police escorted me to packed meetings in cafeterias, where the public asked questions and took positions about who was responsible and what should happen next. It was hatred unleashed.

The other superintendents called me to join them for lunch, offering me respite. At the end of the day, I would hug my golden retriever and read myself this poem. Pain passes as all things do. I could fall asleep, holding hope. In the spring, they dedicated a garden to her in front of the school.

—*Ann Myers*

Ann Myers has been an educator for nearly forty years. Formerly a superintendent, she is now an associate professor in the School of Education and director of the Educational Leadership Program at the Sage Colleges in upstate New York.

For the raindrop, joy is in entering the river

For the raindrop, joy is in entering the river—
Unbearable pain becomes its own cure.

Travel far enough into sorrow, tears turn to sighing;
In this way we learn how water can die into air.

When, after heavy rain, the stormclouds disperse,
Is it not that they've wept themselves clear to the end?

If you want to know the miracle, how wind can polish a mirror,
Look: the shining grass grows green in spring.

It's the rose's unfolding, Ghalib, that creates the desire to see—
In every color and circumstance, may the eyes be open for what
    comes.

—Ghalib

This poem names the twin pillars of despair and hope that I stand between as a lawyer and a leader. Mary Oliver does not try to soften the harsh realities of the "black rain water" drowning many of us in our maddening vocational pursuits. So often I have felt a heaviness in my bones, seeking meaning in a profession that many lawyers—and the clients they serve—believe has lost its moral compass.

When I fall prey to the crippling forces of cynicism and disillusionment, I am emboldened by the vision of young Blake, who saw God come "fluttering up" through the window of the factory. I am able to turn from despair to hope when I remember the wings I stand on—the mentors who encouraged me to stay true to my passion to pursue law as a calling to serve those most in need. Every day my board members inspire me with their bold belief that law is a vehicle for healing. And the unprecedented outpouring of pro bono legal support from thousands of lawyers in the aftermath of Hurricane Katrina, with its raw exposure of unthinkable injustice, has rekindled my faith in the profession.

Leadership for change starts with imagining a new reality—for ourselves, our institutions, and our communities. Each lawyer I meet who has turned away from darkness to live into a new vision for the profession is a blue ribbon of flame. That keeps me soaring.

—*Bonnie Allen*

Bonnie Allen is president of the Center for Law & Renewal. She has held senior management positions at the American Bar Association and National Legal Aid and Defender Association. Allen practiced law in Florida early in her career, and she holds a law degree and a master's degree in theological studies.

Spring Azures

In spring the blue azures bow down
at the edges of shallow puddles
to drink the black rain water.
Then they rise and float away into the
    fields.

Sometimes the great bones of my life feel so
    heavy,
and all the tricks my body knows—
the opposable thumbs, the kneecaps,
and the mind clicking and clicking—

don't seem enough to carry me through this
    world
and I think: how I would like

to have wings—
blue ones—
ribbons of flame.

How I would like to open them, and rise
from the black rain water.

And then I think of Blake, in the dirt and
    sweat of London—a boy
staring through the window, when God
    came
fluttering up.

Of course, he screamed,
seeing the bobbin of God's blue body
leaning on the sill,
and the thousand-faceted eyes.

Well, who knows.
Who knows what hung, fluttering, at the
    window
between him and the darkness.

Anyway, Blake the hosier's son stood up
and turned away from the sooty sill and the
    dark city—
turned away forever
from the factories, the personal strivings,

to a life of the imagination.

—*Mary Oliver*

I am a Catholic priest, the pastor of a parish. I have been a spiritual leader in the ministry for forty-five years. Once someone asked me, "Do you ever experience burnout?" I said, "Yes, about twice a day. Once before lunch, again in the afternoon."

My lowest point was in the 1980s. I had become a priest to make a difference, and I did not see it happening. I tried to carry a message that joy, happiness, and life comes from within us. Yet the message of the world and the T.V. is that joy comes from the outside and happiness comes from things. It is hard to compete, and I was not coping; I felt no hope.

In this low point, I realized some things. God was closer to me when I was low than when I was in control. When I was at my worst, I was very close to being at my best. God was close and that presence was what I needed.

People are always searching for God. They talk about it; they write books about it. William Blake believed that imagination was a surer guide to truth than reason or common sense. The sources of life are within us, in our imagination. We only have to see rightly.

My calling is not to teach but to model. I realized that if I could stay intensely alive, I could show others the way.

And William Blake shows us the way, the way of wonder, the way of a child.

—James O'Leary

James O'Leary is pastor of a small parish in Parchment, Michigan. He writes: "I was born with two companions, sisters. We are triplets. This has added a dimension of richness to my life. I find a great deal of joy here. I am 71 and hope to keep working into my 80s."

From "Auguries of Innocence"

To see a world in a Grain of Sand
And a Heaven in a Wild Flower
Hold Infinity in the palm of your hand
And Eternity in an hour.

—William Blake

"A low spot where horizon disappears"—how often in the course of thirty years as a small-business leader this has been my reality! As the person "in charge," surely I must know where we're going and how we're going to get there. But frequently I do not.

As I read the words of this poem, a feeling of release resonates in my soul. It advises me to stop paddling so furiously, take a breath, and survey my surroundings. On a deeper level it touches a raw core of loneliness that I carry—a burden that I've placed heavily upon my shoulders. It's the erroneous but very persistent story I tell myself that I alone must find a way to make "everything" work. The buck stops here; it's ultimately all on my plate. I must work harder.

This poem whispers to my weary heart that I am but a small part of the equation. Much larger forces are at work. Faith in the powerful natural cycle of water and waves is what is really called for. It asks me to believe I can work in harmony with that rhythm rather than always trying to push through it.

As I try to imagine the sensation of floating between huge waves, I wait to see not where I want to swim; I imagine myself swimming where I "need to swim." The weight of decision making floats off my shoulders. Instead, by some wise and mysterious process I don't even understand, the path becomes clear.

—Linda Wolfe

Linda Wolfe is the co-owner of the Smile Herb Shop, "An Emporium for Healthful Living," serving a broad community of people across wide economic diversities, offering in-depth guidance and products to consumers interested in holistic health. Recently, she has focused on the development of an extensive educational e-commerce site [www.smileherb.com].

Trough

There is a trough in waves,
a low spot
where horizon disappears
and only sky
and water
are our company.

And there we lose our way
unless
we rest, knowing the wave will bring us
to its crest again.

There we may drown
if we let fear
hold us within its grip and shake us
side to side,
and leave us flailing, torn, disoriented.

But if we rest there
in the trough,
in silence,
being with
the low part of the wave,
keeping
our energy and
noticing the shape of things,
the flow,
then time alone
will bring us to another
place
where we can see
horizon, see the land again,
regain our sense
of where
we are,
and where we need to swim.

—*Judy Brown*

I have practiced medicine for almost twenty years. During that time I have become a mother, a young widow, and a wife for the second time. In the year following my first husband's death, I continued to practice obstetrics and gynecology, even though some nights I covered my head with blankets and sobbed my loss and desolation into the pillow after putting my five-year-old daughter to sleep. I'd swallow my tears when my pager went off and answer the summons to the hospital to care for others. Loving my daughter and loving my patients was what kept me alive in those dark days.

This fragment of a longer poem by the Sufi poet Rumi means much to me. A turning point in my healing came when I realized that I had not been singled out for especially rotten treatment and that my experience of personal grief was part of the universal experience of being human. I have no illusions of wholeness. I know that I am wounded. My wounds are like familiar companions, and I accept the truth of them in myself and in others. But strangely, I also know that a place exists inside me, deeper than the wounds, that is untouched by pain and loss. It's that part of each of us that is transcendent, and I recognize it in even my sickest patients.

I am humbled by my patients and their strength. It is a mystery that I carry with me in my work each day: who is broken, and who is whole?

—*Karen E. Adams, M.D.*

Karen E. Adams, M.D., began college as a violin performance major, attained a B.S. in psychology with honors, and is now associate professor and residency program director of obstetrics and gynecology at Oregon Health and Sciences University. She codirects The Healer's Art, a medical school course dedicated to reclaiming the spirit of service in medicine.

From "Childhood Friends"

Trust your wound to a teacher's surgery
Flies collect on a wound. They cover it,
those flies of your self-protecting feelings,
your love for what you think is yours.

Let a teacher wave away the flies
and put a plaster on the wound.

Don't turn your head. Keep looking
at the bandaged place. That's where
the light enters you.
                    And don't believe for a moment
that you're healing yourself.

                                        —*Rumi*

My life is held by the love of a mother who, despite limited opportunities and deferred dreams, dared to believe, care, and act for the sake of her soul and the soul of her children and community.

The humble language of "Mother to Son" speaks to me in times of failure and disillusionment, as well as times of accomplishments and acceptance. As an organizer and facilitator, I often find my best work happens when the meeting is over.

Once I hosted a series of meetings of central city Fort Worth neighbors to share ideas to improve their community. The ground rules were simple: be kind, listen well, and speak from your heart. We focused on two questions: (1) what kind of place do I dream of for those I love? (2) what do I love doing? After people read and reflected on their responses, which were posted on the wall, I invited them to speak about what they felt inspired to do. A community garden, voter registration rallies, predatory lending protests, and a neighborhood association all grew from those simple conversations. I remember a young man saying, "When people listened to me I felt like I was somebody worth hearing. When people trusted me I felt trustworthy. When you open your heart first and then open your eyes, you see people and places differently. We had many gifts, we just didn't see them."

Seeing these people take action, I "don't turn back" but dare to believe, to care, and to act just as my mother did, taking on life as she found it.

—Estrus Tucker

Estrus Tucker is president/CEO of Liberation Community, Inc., a social-justice advocacy organization, and has served in the nonprofit community leadership field for over twenty-five years. He is a keynote speaker encouraging nonviolent activism, civic integrity, and compassion, in service of a world that works for all.

Mother to Son

Well, son, I'll tell you:
Life for me ain't been no crystal stair.
It's had tacks in it,
And splinters,
And boards torn up,
And places with no carpet on the floor—
Bare.
But all the time
I'se been a-climbin' on,
And reachin' landin's,
And turnin' corners,
And sometimes goin' in the dark
Where there ain't been no light.
So boy, don't you turn back.
Don't you set down on the steps.
'Cause you finds it's kinder hard.
Don't you fall now—
For I'se still goin', honey,
I'se still climbin',
And life for me ain't been no crystal stair.

—Langston Hughes

I am a choreographer who believes that radical acts of art can happen in all kinds of places. My work with the Dance Exchange takes me to beautiful stages and to shipyards, science labs, and synagogues. After thirty years of this work, I am no longer surprised when I discover that geneticists love metaphor or that ancient institutions welcome cutting-edge ideas.

I work collaboratively with a wonderful group of dancers, a capable staff, and a smart board of advisers, but I often feel the isolation and exhaustion of being out in front of a long-surviving nonprofit. I resonate with the words Yehuda Amichai uses to open each stanza, as they reflect a part of my everyday, insomniac life: "I'm tired. . . . I'm tired and curse."

What a description of the nature of leadership. It doesn't matter whether the battles are about money, or people, or the intractable stubbornness of the creative journey. Somewhere along the way comes that moment when I wish I had not chosen this, when I just want a simple job where someone else tells me what to do. Instead, I get not one wrestling match but thousands, sometimes simultaneously.

The poet does not promise us success or respite. He simply says we shall be ready or not. But he also tells us about how joyful we can be in knowing that we can and will always reach.

It is not always this difficult. Days and months of relative calm pass by. But then someone puts down the wrestling mat and we begin again. God, let the world rest. Please.

—*Liz Lerman*

Liz Lerman is a choreographer, educator, speaker, writer, and founding artistic director of the Liz Lerman Dance Exchange. Described by the *Washington Post* as "the source of an epochal revolution in the scope and purpose of dance art," she has received numerous honors, including a 2002 MacArthur "Genius Grant" Fellowship.

End of Elul

I'm tired of the summer. The smoke near the monastery of the silent nuns
Is all I have to say. This year, the winter
Will be late, when we shall be ready for it and shall not be.

I'm tired and curse the three famous religions
That won't let me sleep at night, with bells
And yells, pesty shofars and lamentations.

God, close your houses, let the world rest,
Why didn't You forsake me? The year is hesitant this year.
The summer goes on. If not for the tears
I amassed all those years, I would have dried with the thorns.

Great battles continue inside me in terrible silence,
Only the sighs, as of thousands of wrestlers, naked
And sweating. Not iron or stone, just flesh fighting like serpents.
Then they will fall off each other in passion,
And from the exhaustion, there will be clouds
And rain, when we shall be ready and shall not be.

—*Yehuda Amichai*

I remember when I was a little kid in St. Paul, Minnesota, there was a "Lost and Found" department in one of the big stores downtown. It was reassuring then that "lost" and "found" were paired. Fortunately, they still are.

Even now—maybe even more so, as the president of a foundation—the question is not whether I'll get lost but how do I live when I get lost. The first step toward finding my way is to recognize that I am lost—lost in fear, in self-doubt and pity, lost in my own stuff.

"Lost" for me is when I separate from what I know to be true about myself. I become blind to my shadows and wall myself off from others. When I'm lost, I can do real damage. Internally, I give in to guilt, loneliness, and defensiveness. Externally, I'll blame someone else for my lost-ness, spreading uncertainty and resentment among my colleagues, friends, and loved ones.

The next step toward finding my way is to loosen up, to lighten up, to "know to wait" and to "know to risk." Sometimes, I begin to find my way with my own resources, by taking a deep breath so that I stop thrashing around. Sometimes quiet meditation leads to "that special calm." More often, though, someone will reach through the wall I've built and, with a soft touch, a gentle or forceful word, help me find my way home.

This poem reminds me that I'm never ultimately or irreparably lost. "Lost" and "found" are always paired.

—Tom Beech

Tom Beech is president and CEO of the Fetzer Institute. Before joining the Institute, he was executive director of The Minneapolis Foundation and executive vice president and CEO of The Burnett Foundation. He has served on the boards of directors of the Council on Foundations and the Independent Sector.

When You Get Lost

Tell me what you do
when you get lost
Tell me

Tell me what you feel
How things look to you
What happens in your head
What you say to yourself
Tell me

Can you see anything
when you get lost
Can you hear what's about you
Do you perceive life at all
Tell me

Tell me what scares you most
when you get lost
Can you draw from deep inside
What you use to hold you up
Do you move yourself differently
Tell me

Tell me what you do
to reach that special calm
Can you direct a prayer
When do you know to wait
When do you know to risk
Tell me

Tell me what you do
when you get lost
Tell me

Then tell me
How you know
When you not lost
no more
Tell me

—*Carol Prejean Zippert*

I run a program for students with emotional and behavioral problems. My staff and I struggle to build relationships with these long-wounded and rejected students. Feeling hopeless and powerless, the students often thrash out aggressively. Any of us can show compassion at times, but my staff must continually provide unyielding emotional support, protection, and forgiveness to these mistrusting students. Occasionally, the staff feels discouraged and may be tempted to return student aggression with counter-aggression particularly when their students reject their care and concern.

I recall a day when Nancy, one of my most skilled teachers, came to my office. I could tell from her face that she was beyond tears and darkness was setting in. She told me that one of her adolescent girls was extremely abusive toward her during class. The verbal barrage had touched Nancy's own unhealed wounds. This was not the time for me to share a new intervention strategy from the principal's bag of tricks. Instead, I shared that often I feel like Sisyphus slogging up a mountain, only to be pushed back by adversity and self-doubt. When I feel myself sinking into my own darkness and discouragement, I turn to Henri Nouwen and strive to work around my abyss to refocus and to bring a bit of healing and renewal.

Nancy took my book; several days later she returned and said that she was again holding both the pain and the hope, and smiled as she returned to class.

—*John Marston*

John Marston has over thirty years of experience as a principal, administrator, and special education teacher. He is administrator of Alternative Schools and Character Education for the Fairfax County Public Schools, an adjunct professor at the University of Virginia and The George Washington University, and a Courage & Renewal facilitator.

Work Around Your Abyss

There is a deep hole in your being, like an abyss. You will never succeed in filling that hole, because your needs are inexhaustible. You have to work around it so that gradually the abyss closes.

Since the hole is so enormous and your anguish so deep, you will always be tempted to flee from it. There are two extremes to avoid: being completely absorbed in your pain and being distracted by so many things that you stay far away from the wound you want to heal.

—Henry Nouwen

As a Hispanic physician of African descent, it is difficult to sustain my optimism. Each day I encounter at least one patient who has no health insurance or who needs a medication that is not covered by insurance. I see children who go to school ill because both parents work and children who could have been treated by a school nurse if only the school district could afford this service.

Taking care of others provides few immediate rewards. I often delay gratification and work toward long-term goals. I frequently forget to celebrate today's accomplishments or to reach out to others and ask them for help.

How do I continue? I tell myself "like kidney stones, this too shall pass." I try to take comfort in the work my colleagues and I are doing to provide quality health care for all populations. As a medical educator, I find solace in knowing that we are launching exquisitely competent physicians who are healers, scientists, and advocates. And I look for poems that inspire or calm me, or both, as it is in that calm that I do my best work as a physician and teacher.

Poetry is not only about words that speak to my soul; it is also about rhythm and song. I therefore often choose poetry written in my first language, Spanish. I start my staff meetings each week with a poem. During the silence that follows, I watch as someone takes a deep breath or smiles, appearing more ready for the "new day" as physician, teacher, healer.

—Sandra P. Daley

Sandra P. Daley has been a pediatrician for thirty years and a professor of pediatrics at the University of California, San Diego School of Medicine, for fifteen years. As assistant dean of diversity, she is responsible for programs that help students from educationally disadvantaged backgrounds seek admission to health professions schools.

Amanecer

Hincho mi corazón para que entre
como cascada ardiente el Universo.
El nuevo día llega y su llegada
me deja sin aliento.
Canto como la gruta que es colmada
canto mi día nuevo.

Por la gracia perdida y recobrada
humilde soy sin dar y recibiendo
hasta que la Gorgona de la noche
va, derrotada, huyendo.

Daybreak

My heart swells that the Universe
like a fiery cascade may enter.
The new day comes. Its coming
leaves me breathless.
I sing. Like a cavern brimming
I sing my new day.

For grace lost and recovered
I stand humble. Not giving. Receiving.
Until the Gorgon night,
vanquished, flees.

—*Gabriela Mistral*

Today, all the good people are exhausted.

The teachers, parents, community leaders, social workers, doctors, clergy, nurses—those who keep our dreams alive, keep us drenched in hope, faith, and courage—they are overwhelmed, exhausted, and discouraged. We are all painfully aware of how little we have to offer, given the weight and magnitude of the sorrow, injustice, or pain we are to witness and heal.

Doctors believe they have not healed enough; parents ache for not better protecting their children; community leaders cannot stand up for one more fight; nurses wish they could care more than their sixty-hour week allows; clergy are ashamed for not healing enough fractured, lonely souls.

This is our challenge: What is enough?

After two life-threatening illnesses, I have learned to move slowly, to need and accept care, to remember the miraculous nourishment of the kind word, the hand upon hand, the simple company of two hearts breaking together. Jesus said, "Pay attention to the small things, how they grow." The mustard seed, the leaven in the bread, the pearl of great price—these, he said, are the small, simple seeds of heaven on earth.

Now, when I speak with groups of good-hearted community leaders and healers, I ask of us only this: Remember how small things grow. We cannot heal it all. But as my dear friend Mark Nepo writes, "We can feed each other." We can offer small, nearly invisible kindnesses that take flight into some resplendent future, effortless, alive.

This is what we can do.

—*Wayne Muller*

Wayne Muller is an ordained minister, therapist, and author. He is founder of Bread for the Journey, a national, nonprofit charity nurturing grassroots, neighborhood philanthropy. He is a recipient of the 2007 Temple Award for Creative Altruism and the author of *How, Then, Shall We Live?*

Accepting This

Yes, it is true. I confess,
I have thought great thoughts,
and sung great songs—all of it
rehearsal for the majesty
of being held.

The dream is awakened
when thinking I love you
and life begins
when saying I love you
and joy moves like blood
when embracing others with love.

My efforts now turn
from trying to outrun suffering
to accepting love wherever
I can find it.

Stripped of causes and plans
and things to strive for,
I have discovered everything
I could need or ask for
is right here—
in flawed abundance.

We cannot eliminate hunger,
but we can feed each other.
We cannot eliminate loneliness,
but we can hold each other.
We cannot eliminate pain,
but we can live a life
of compassion.

Ultimately,
we are small living things
awakened in the stream,
not gods who carve out rivers.

Like human fish,
we are asked to experience
meaning in the life that moves
through the gill of our heart.

There is nothing to do
and nowhere to go.
Accepting this,
we can do everything
and go anywhere.

—*Mark Nepo*

Pay Attention

$\mathcal{E}$ verybody wants a piece of the leader. Whether you're in charge of a sprawling, global corporation, an urban ministry, a hospital clinic, or the parent-teacher organization at your neighborhood school, one must learn to handle the overload of information, requests, and demands. From paperwork, to unending e-mails, to revolving meetings, the challenge is to attend to the details while staying connected to larger purposes.

Busyness comes with the territory of leadership and it's critical for leaders to learn how to manage the precious resource of attention. Paying attention, leaders told us, means that before venturing out and engaging the stimuli of the outside world, leaders must venture inward—before action comes listening. It means taking a moment, as the poet David Wagoner describes, to "stand still . . . listen," for in that space you will find images of what's possible so that you can reach out, engage the unknown, connect, and challenge convention.

After paying attention to self, to others, to the great needs in the world, you are better poised to experiment, to resist the status quo, to take risks, and to encourage others. With vision and hunch in hand and heart, leaders must trust their core and believe in their truth, their intuition, and their inner teacher. These stories and poems of leadership portray leaders answering the question Pablo Neruda puts to us: "Whom can I ask what I came/to make happen in this world?"

For over a quarter of a century, I have worked with people in all sorts of work settings to discover and deepen their connection with what matters most in their lives and to build organizations that honor and nurture this connection— something continually eroded by the never-ending fire drill that defines most professionals' daily lives.

This was expressed beautifully by a woman from AT&T in a session with David Whyte:

> Ten years ago. . . .
> I turned my face for a moment
> And it became my life.

It is no coincidence that when our lives are fragmented, our organizations and the larger social and natural systems of which they are a part suffer. The problem is that we stop paying attention. More to the point, we forget what to pay attention to.

To create institutions, from school to work, that do not predispose us to "turn our faces," we must start with truisms central to native traditions. Nature is incapable of producing two identical creations, and she calls us to discover and bring forth our uniqueness. The great mystery is that life, too, colludes in finding us. We would never think of a tree or a branch as being lost. Why would we be different? It is only through forgetting that we are expressions of the same source that we delude ourselves into thinking otherwise.

How long will it take to find our way back to "Here"? How long will it take to let go of the delusion of separateness so that we can learn to live together differently?

—Peter Senge

Peter Senge is founding chair of the Society for Organizational Learning (SoL) Council. A senior lecturer at MIT, he is the author of *The Fifth Discipline* and lectures throughout the world about decentralizing the role of leadership in organizations to enhance the capacity of all people to work toward healthier human systems.

Lost

Stand Still. The trees ahead and bushes besides you
Are not lost. Wherever you are is called Here,
And you must treat it as a powerful stranger,
Must ask permission to know it and be known.
The forest breathes. Listen. It answers,
I have made this place around you.
If you leave it, you may come back again, saying Here.
No two trees are the same to Raven.
No two branches are the same to Wren.
If what a tree or a bush does is lost on you,
You are surely lost. Stand still. The forest knows
Where you are. You must let it find you.

—*David Wagoner*

As an overachieving son of an overachieving father, imperfection was a skill I never learned. I went to the right schools and got the right grades. Leaving for college I was destined to become a successful businessman on Wall Street.

I think I was as surprised as anyone my senior year when I walked out of an investment banking interview and into the ministry. I knew I had the drive to succeed in the ministry, but that soon surfaced as the problem. All I knew how to do was achieve, and that didn't count when caring for souls.

After two ill-fated ministry assignments—first as a chaplain to boarding school students in New England and then as a missionary to garbage dump dwellers in Mexico City—I stumbled back to the States in need of soul repair. Since I'd never looked deeply into myself, I found I had little depth to bring to others. That's when someone gave me Rilke's poem.

The next five years I spent my Saturday mornings in a little garden reciting Rilke's prayer at the foot of a piece of granite. That sculpture might as well have been my soul—a robed man folded over himself, hunkered down against the world.

I've moved cities since then, but somehow that sculpture and that poem moved inside with me. From inside, they unlocked the kind of vulnerability and imperfection that set hearts free. Now, ten years later, I'm writing from that little garden; I'm still unfolding, and I'm still in ministry.

—Bill White

Bill White has been in the ministry since 1990. He and his wife, Katy, and their two children live in urban Los Angeles, where she serves as a physician in a community clinic and he serves as the outreach pastor for Emmanuel Church.

From "I am too alone in the world, and not alone enough"

I want to unfold
I don't want to stay folded anywhere,
because where I am folded, there I am a lie.
And I want my grasp of things
true before you. I want to describe myself
like a painting that I looked at
closely for a long time,
like a saying that I finally understood,
like the pitcher I use every day,
like the face of my mother,
like a ship
that took me safely
through the wildest storm of all.

—*Rainer Maria Rilke*

I suppose there's something in the DNA of institutions that requires strategic planning, marketing analysis, and plotting the future in five-year increments. As a graduate school administrator, I do my share of assessing, prioritizing, reporting. After all, I certainly want to be part of a productive, mission-driven organization.

Or do I? Hmmm. Do I want to be driven by anything, including mission? Or do I want to be fluent, as John O'Donohue describes in this small jewel of a poem?

When I'm tempted to lead by rote, by technique, or, worse, by someone else's compass, this poem reminds me of the way the river has to trust its own unfolding. No leader can see the end from the beginning, no matter how strategic the plan. Lake Itasca, the source of the Mississippi River, cannot imagine New Orleans.

Leadership by "unfolding" is something I've come to relatively late in life. I spent years heeding others with more experience, more credentials, or simply more volume. But with the support and grace of friends and colleagues, I began to trust my vision, my truth, my intuition. I began to see the invitations inherent in leadership, not just the demands. Now, when momentum or deadlines push for making controversial decisions quickly, I request time for reflection. I encourage members of my team to pay attention to their own inner truth, and the gifts of insight they offer add to the river's unfolding, taking us places the five-year plan could not have imagined.

—Carla M. Dahl

Carla M. Dahl has been a psychotherapist for twenty-six years, a mother for twenty-four, and a professor of marriage and family studies for sixteen. She is currently the dean of the Center for Spiritual and Personal Formation at Bethel Seminary, where she directs the training program in marriage and family therapy.

Amidst the memorabilia and readings spread throughout my office is a window to the outside world. It looks out on one of the most spectacular bodies of water: the San Francisco Bay. Despite the breathtaking view, the window has long since been covered with the expressions of who I am: a statement of purpose, a prayer on the importance of silence, children's art, and quotes that have touched my soul. The centerpiece of this makeshift collage is the "Tao Ching #33," which was the first piece I hung on the window over ten years ago.

The fact that this poem is the centerpiece is an apt metaphor for how we should embrace the world. If we go outside ourselves, we will see the world. However, to understand ourselves, we must look inside, which is far more demanding than looking at the outside world. Looking inside means disengaging from the distractions that encumber our daily lives.

I started my career as a physician but soon learned that to touch many lives I needed to work on healing the medical system. Healing the system meant shifting my work from caring for individuals to training doctors and clinicians, devising interventions to deal with the growing numbers of uninsured, and developing innovative best practices related to hospital governance.

When I enter my office, I know the daily challenge for me is not to see the outside world but to try to stay in the center so that I can endure and do the work that calls me.

—*Kevin Fickenscher, M.D.*

Kevin Fickenscher, M.D., is a physician executive and leader with extensive experience in complex health care organizations. He is executive vice president for Healthcare Transformation at Perot Systems, and his mission is to make a difference in the lives of people by working diligently to improve the human condition.

Tao Ching #33

Knowing others is intelligence;
knowing yourself is true wisdom.
Mastering others is strength;
mastering yourself is true power.

If you realize that you have enough
you are truly rich.
If you stay in the center
and embrace death with your whole heart,
you will endure forever.

I was in my second year of pediatric training when I was led to save a young girl's life. We were in the emergency department, and she had fallen asleep while waiting to be transported to her room. While I was writing my notes, something turned me around and walked me over to lift her eyelids. She had "blown a pupil"—an early sign of brain herniation.

Seven years in medical school and residency training embedded me in the measurable truths of science. My natural tendency to look at the world through a spiritual lens submerged under its incisive certitudes. Yet moments of grace continued to come unbidden, persistent in their call to return to what I once knew.

Later, working with physicians about their own well-being, I found I was not alone. Physicians were yearning, as David Whyte writes, to open their eyes and listen again to their hearts. To walk beside someone in the intimacy of what gives life and what brings death is a sacred act and a great privilege. We see our patients most truly in their illnesses through the wisdom and clarity of our own hearts and souls. This poem came to me at a critical juncture in my work, a time when I could have turned to the call of my heart or let its whisperings fall deeper into silence. I return to it when I need reminding that listening to my heart and being open to receive grace is my truest way of being.

—*Hanna B. Sherman, M.D.*

Hanna B. Sherman, M.D., is an educator and consultant who works with physicians and health care leaders to develop sustaining professional careers and relationship-centered organizations. Her work includes leadership development, based on teachings from diverse wisdom traditions. She directs courses on professional renewal for the American Academy on Communication in Healthcare.

The Opening of Eyes

That day I saw beneath dark clouds
the passing light over the water
and I heard the voice of the world speak out,
I knew then, as I had before
life is no passing memory of what has been
nor the remaining pages in a great book
waiting to be read.

It is the opening of eyes long closed.
It is the vision of far off things
seen for the silence they hold.
It is the heart after years
of secret conversing
speaking out loud in the clear air.

It is Moses in the desert
fallen to his knees before the lit bush.
It is the man throwing away his shoes
as if to enter heaven
and finding himself astonished,
opened at last,
fallen in love with solid ground.

—*David Whyte*

Against the backdrop of 9/11, the wars in Afghanistan and Iraq, terrorism, torture, insurgencies, counter-insurgencies, Guantanamo Bay, and Abu Ghraib, to name but a few, I teach ethics to midshipmen at the U.S. Naval Academy. I do my best to impart to them a sense that no matter how difficult it may be, no matter how great the pressures or temptations, they must not surrender their honor or integrity or allow those they lead to do so either.

Here I have found the writings of the Stoics, with their emphasis on the freedom and responsibility of the individual to choose his response regardless of the circumstance, of central importance. But initially this ancient and somewhat obscure philosophy was not well received by the midshipmen; it was seemingly too distant and removed from their lives to be of any concern. I struggled to make this material come alive.

Then a naval officer—a SEAL with whom I had previously team-taught—asked if I knew of the poem "Invictus." I said that I had, that it was one of my favorites but had not thought of using it. Thanks to his prompting, however, I now conclude every fall and spring by reading "Invictus."

In lecture halls of more than one hundred students you can literally hear a pin drop as I read the final stanza: "It matters not how strait the gate,/How charged with punishments the scroll,/I am the master of my fate:/I am the captain of my soul."

—David J. Garren

David J. Garren is an associate professor of philosophy at the U.S. Naval Academy. He is also founder and faculty representative for the Naval Academy Socratic Society, a philosophy club that provides an informal forum for the exploration of philosophical questions.

Invictus

Out of the night that covers me,
    Black as the Pit from pole to pole,
I thank whatever gods may be
    For my unconquerable soul.

In the fell clutch of circumstance
    I have not winced nor cried aloud.
Under the bludgeonings of chance
    My head is bloody, but unbowed.

Beyond this place of wrath and tears
    Looms but the Horror of the shade,
And yet the menace of the years
    Finds, and shall find, me unafraid.

It matters not how strait the gate,
    How charged with punishments the scroll,
I am the master of my fate:
    I am the captain of my soul.

—*William Ernest Henley*

I became a church musician when I was old enough for my feet to touch the pedals of the piano. Since then I have played hymns in small country churches and large ecumenical forums. I've accompanied cantors and choirs, soloists and stage performers from behind old uprights, as well as in the sheltering wing of a big black grand. Accompanying others is one thing I believe I really know how to do.

Now, staring deep into the yawn of midlife, I reflect on a journey of leadership in the shadows: always the accompanist, seldom the bride. The blues-like rhythm of confession and hope emanating from this poem is my lifeline for finding my own voice in the second half of life.

I know I am not alone in this search. I have seen how this poem gives courage to those starting out or starting over. For me, leaving a church musician job after more than twenty years of service has given me true Sabbath Sundays to reflect on my voice as an accompanist and embrace it in a new way. These days I find myself playing solo as I look out my window, trying to "find truth in my own backyard." Contrary to craving some elusive limelight, finding my own voice now means losing it: leaving the familiar routine, while not yet knowing the next step. This is a time for "bandaging knees" and letting the music of life breathe.

It's a good time to let this poem be my accompanist for a while.

—Karen Lee Turner

Karen Lee Turner teaches in the adult liberal studies program at Belmont University. Her courses focus on helping students live through change and transition, find their voice, and compose lives that matter. She is a contributing author to *Weavings* and has been a pastoral musician for over thirty years.

I'm Tired, I'm Whipped

I'm tired
I'm whipped
too dumb to quit
too smart
to let life go by

I'm working hard
to find truth
in my own backyard
I've done everything
but die

Took the long way around
on a short ride to town
found a pass
where few have been

Gained a love
lost a friend
scraped my knees
learning to please

started out
with no choice

somewhere

somehow

found my
voice

—*Nevin Compton Trammell*

I was introduced to the poetry of Yehuda Amichai in a strange and wonderful college course on modern Hebrew poetry. This was a spontaneous and ironic choice, as I grew up ashamed of my Jewish roots. My mother was a baptized Methodist. My father was raised as a Reform Jew but later was baptized as a Methodist. I was raised in the Unitarian tradition, so I had a mixed religious pedigree in a small upstate New York village populated by unwavering Catholics and Protestants. Not attending church made me feel like an outsider, often uncomfortable in my own skin. I was frequently called "a little Jew boy" by a close family friend. The way this person taunted me with my Jewish background made me feel as though it was something to hide.

Nearly three decades later, I discovered that my great-great grandfather was a prominent rabbi in Buffalo, New York. Part of his legacy was coaxing his traditional congregation to allow women to attend temple and study the Torah and to allow conversions within the synagogue. His was a courageous and revolutionary spirit that I could identify with; it gave me deep pride in my family roots.

This poem speaks to me about how a single action can reverberate with enormous consequences. It reminds me how the life of one child in one classroom can eventually affect the vitality and security of an entire nation—an entire planet. Ultimately, the diameter of a quality public education stretches across all human consciousness.

—Howie Schaffer

Howie Schaffer is the public outreach director of Public Education Network (PEN), an organization working to reform public schools in low-income communities. His main responsibilities include production of the PEN Weekly NewsBlast and serving as PEN's media spokesperson. Prior to PEN, Schaffer worked in various political jobs, including campaign and legislative work.

The Diameter of the Bomb

The diameter of the bomb was thirty centimeters
and the diameter of its effective range about seven meters,
with four dead and eleven wounded.
And around these, in a larger circle
of pain and time, two hospitals are scattered
and one graveyard. But the young woman
who was buried in the city she came from,
at a distance of more than a hundred kilometers,
enlarges the circle considerably,
and the solitary man mourning her death
at the distant shores of a country far across the sea
includes the entire world in the circle.
And I won't even mention the howl of orphans
that reaches to the throne of God and
beyond, making
a circle with no end and no God.

—*Yehuda Amichai*

It is said that at one point Rilke could not write. He sought out Rodin, the sculptor, who told him that to write he must first see something clearly. Rodin advised Rilke to go to the zoo and to look at something until he finally really saw it and then write a poem about it. "The Panther" is such a poem.

Pretend her name was Mary Jones. Cocaine addiction, AIDS, and osteomyelitis put her into the hospital; the nurses wanted her out. When last seen she had defecated into her hand, thrown the feces at the nurse, and shouted: "Now you'll get AIDS, too."

I went to see her. "Hello, I'm Doctor Leach and I'm looking for Mary Jones." Her eyes were both fierce and shamed as she snarled, "I'm Mary Jones."

"I don't think you are," I replied. "I have heard that Mary Jones is very sensitive and actually quite nice. I'm looking for her—have you seen her?"

She began to cry; I extended my hand and said, "It's nice to meet you, Ms. Jones. I'm sorry I didn't recognize you." The next morning she had cleaned up her room and herself; she completed the six-week course of treatment and became everyone's favorite patient.

This poem rings true. Mary Jones was pacing behind bars; the medical profession is pacing behind bars. In both cases immense power and beauty are confined and exhausted. Our task is to really see and to act accordingly.

—David C. Leach, M.D.

David C. Leach, M.D., is the executive director of the Accreditation Council for Graduate Medical Education (ACGME). He is interested in using accreditation to foster improvement, build and recognize community, and improve patient care by improving residency education.

The Panther

From seeing the bars, his seeing is so exhausted
that it no longer holds anything anymore.
To him the world is bars, a hundred thousand
bars, and behind the bars, nothing.

The lithe swinging of that rhythmical easy stride
which circles down to the tiniest hub
is like a dance of energy around a point
in which a great will stands stunned and numb.

Only at times the curtains of the pupil rise
without a sound . . . then a shape enters,
slips through the tightened silence of the shoulders,
reaches the heart, and dies.

—*Rainer Maria Rilke*

Back when I was the director of human resources for a midsize corporation, I would often pause as I left for the day, take a look around my office, and ask myself, "Well Lee, are you having fun?"

Amidst the intense demands of the corporate life, the pursuit of "having fun" felt unrealistic, and my query was slightly sarcastic. But I meant it, and the question kept weighing in. Was I making a difference in the world? I still dared to dream of work where I could contribute my ideas, my creative impulses, and my unique slant to things that mattered.

When Sage, our only child, was born, I felt I should keep to the "safer" road and pursue job security. I thought being a reliable father should trump adventure, daring, and jumping off into the unknown. But that is exactly what I did. Why? Because I could not get two questions out of my head: "So how far can you swim, Daddy?" and "Tell me Daddy, did you do what you wanted to do in your life?"

Some day on a distant shore when Sage asks me those questions, I want to be able to tell her the story of how far I swam when I took a leap of faith and left the security of the corporate life to found justCommunity. I want to tell her that I left because I believe children need an organization devoted to asking: What matters to youth? And with that vision, I began to swim.

—Lee Rush

Lee Rush has thirty years' experience in education, human resources management, nonprofit management, and community activism. In 1999, he founded justCommunity, Inc. and serves as its executive director. He is also the executive director of the National Student Assistance Association, a professional advocacy organization working on behalf of Student Assistance Programs.

With Kit, Age 7, At the Beach

We would climb the highest dune,
from there to gaze and come down:
the ocean was performing;
we contributed our climb.

Waves leapfrogged and came
straight out of the storm.
What should our gaze mean?
Kit waited for me to decide.

Standing on such a hill,
what would you tell your child?
That was an absolute vista.
Those waves raced far, and cold.

"How far could you swim, Daddy,
in such a storm?"
"As far as was needed," I said,
and as I talked, I swam.

                    —*William Stafford*

In 1999, I was rolling without wheels, acting without mindfulness, without purpose. Then one day, I received an unexpected call from a twelve-year-old. "Why do you do what you do?" he blurted.

His homework assignment to interview community leaders prompted him to find me in the Yellow Pages. I was leading a community media organization, so talking to funders about "theories of change" and detailed plans had become easy. Yet my answer for the twelve-year-old was a cringe moment of muddled words. I had lost touch with the essence of why I was doing this.

I became resolved to always be ready to answer WDYDWYD? It is a simple question, yet so much depends on it. I tried turning to external authorities—teachers, mentors, pastors—yet the answer was always in my bones. But I needed a blind student to help me see it.

I taught photography to blind students. They used point-and-shoot cameras, asked about their surroundings, felt their subjects with their hands, and listened carefully. One student photographed the cracked sidewalks at her school, sent them to the superintendent as "proof," and asked for them to be fixed. "Since you are sighted," Leuwynda wrote, "you may not notice these cracks. They are a big problem since my white cane gets stuck."

Leuwynda's story is about more than cracks in a sidewalk; it is about all the cracks that go unnoticed. Her story helped me recognize why I do what I do: to see the cracks in the world and help mend them.

—Tony Deifell

Tony Deifell is a social entrepreneur and founding board member for KaBOOM!. He has also taught photography to blind teenagers and published a book of their work called *Seeing Beyond Sight* (www.seeingbeyondsight.org) and created a project that asks people around the world, "Why do you do what you do?" (www.wdydwyd.com)

William Butler Yeats is my favorite poet. It is very hard to choose my favorite poem. Yeats's breadth—from mystic, to Nobel Prize–winning poet, to member of the Irish Senate—is reflected in his expansive works of poetry. But this short Yeats poem I have chosen reflects a deep truth, both human and political, that politicians often forget. Nothing is forever, ever. It is a political, infectious disease to love and believe your laudatory press coverage. None of us escapes the simple truth of the fact that we are all human—a mixture of the great and not-so-great. We all strive mightily, as Teddy Roosevelt said, and fall short. Often the victories are forgotten, and what remains are the half-finished and the misguided attempts at greatness.

A time comes when we seek respite and yearn to be known for the good we have done. The more civilized we have acted, the more tenderly we will be treated by the memories of those who knew us well.

This poem's beauty is that a widely known street truth—be careful who you step on on the way up, because you may meet them on the way down—can be turned into exquisite poetry.

—Jim McDermott

Jim McDermott, after completing medical residency and military service, served in the Washington State legislature for seventeen years. Then in 1987, he became a Foreign Service medical officer based in Zaire, providing psychiatric services to Foreign Service, AID, and Peace Corps personnel. Since 1989, he has served as congressman from the 7th district of Washington.

The Lover pleads with his Friend for Old Friends

Though you are in your shining days,
Voices among the crowd
And new friends busy with your praise,
Be not unkind or proud,
But think about old friends the most:
Time's bitter flood will rise,
Your beauty perish and be lost
For all eyes but these eyes.

—*William Butler Yeats*

On the hard days, I put on a crisp dress shirt and cinch my tie all the way up. The clothes are my Bat Suit—impersonal and impenetrable. I become the Administrator. I am ready to face the angry parent, confront a wayward teacher, or lead a contentious department meeting.

Give me lunch duties, drug busts, and class cuts!

Then, as I reprimand the ten thousandth teen for the ten thousandth time for being—well, for being a teen—I realize I am tired and depressed.

The problem with the Bat Suit is that it is a Bat Suit—impersonal and impenetrable.

I stopped teaching full time and became an administrator at age twenty-seven. I am now thirty, and I keep a copy of "Mending Wall" in the top left-hand drawer of my desk. When I am tempted to don the Bat Suit, I try to recall Frost's words.

Frost depicts me as weak and fragile; I am the "old-stone savage armed." I feel I must live the archetype of the dominant stony administrator. I fear my youth and my inexperience. I fear not knowing. In those moments, I can't go behind my "father's sayings."

Frost reminds me to free the side of me that is the impetuous speaker of his poem and challenge the walls of my other self. Frost tells me to be the administrator who is the Teacher first and foremost, to see discipline and tough meetings and angry parents as valuable opportunities to learn and teach. I remember. I am rejuvenated. I loosen my tie.

—Adam Bunting

Adam Bunting is an administrator, English teacher, and lacrosse coach at Champlain Valley Union High School in Vermont. Although Bunting is proud to label himself as an educator, he is most pleased to call himself a father and a husband.

Mending Wall

Something there is that doesn't love a wall,
That sends the frozen-ground-swell under it
And spills the upper boulders in the sun,
And makes gaps even two can pass abreast.
The work of hunters is another thing:
I have come after them and made repair
Where they have left not one stone on a stone,
But they would have the rabbit out of hiding,
To please the yelping dogs. The gaps I mean,
No one has seen them made or heard them made,
But at spring mending-time we find them there.
I let my neighbor know beyond the hill;
And on a day we meet to walk the line
And set the wall between us once again.
We keep the wall between us as we go.
To each the boulders that have fallen to each.
And some are loaves and some so nearly balls
We have to use a spell to make them balance:
"Stay where you are until our backs are turned!"
We wear our fingers rough with handling them.
Oh, just another kind of outdoor game,
One on a side. It comes to little more:
There where it is we do not need the wall:
He is all pine and I am apple orchard.
My apple trees will never get across
And eat the cones under his pines, I tell him.
He only says,"Good fences make good neighbors."
Spring is the mischief in me, and I wonder
If I could put a notion in his head:

"*Why* do they make good neighbors? Isn't it
Where there are cows? But here there are no cows.
Before I built a wall I'd ask to know
What I was walling in or walling out,
And to whom I was like to give offense.
Something there is that doesn't love a wall,
That wants it down." I could say "Elves" to him,
But it's not elves exactly, and I'd rather
He said it for himself. I see him there,
Bringing a stone grasped firmly by the top
In each hand, like an old-stone savage armed.
He moves in darkness as it seems to me,
Not of woods only and the shade of trees.
He will not go behind his father's saying,
And he likes having thought of it so well
He says again, "Good fences make good neighbors."

—*Robert Frost*

The Real Bottom Line

The work of leadership takes place in a world driven by outcomes and rational flow charts: profits to be reaped, elections to be won, test scores to be raised, and pews to be filled. The metrics of the bottom line—often precise and narrow—can become the measure of what it means to lead. Performance matters. Measuring up matters. Yet some outcomes elude counting and have to do with what is right, what is just, and what is decent.

Leaders in this section look deeper at the question of what constitutes success and results. What does the bottom line really mean? Where can one find the courage to ease out the difference between performing for the accountant and yearning to do what is right?

The stories and commentaries in this section tell of leaders who struggle to stay focused on alternative bottom lines. They tell us of the anguish of losing an election but finding strength in the notion that a movement is brewing—how they have strived to be a CEO accountable to both the gyrating, urgent short-term expectations of the investors and the long-term view of sustainability within their community.

"Leadership tries its little heart out to be rational," one contributor tells us. But in truth, the formula for the real bottom line must be calculated, as the poet Charles Simic tells us, by the "strange writing, the star charts/on the inner walls."

I have been involved with disability rights groups for many years. I have an adult son who had epilepsy as a child, and I have a twenty-two-year-old son with autism.

I've been a corporate executive for twenty years; for the past fifteen years I have been an author and consultant on the general subjects of leadership and organizational development. In these roles, I face, again and again, people who seem obsessed with the Great God of Productivity. They strive for "excellence"; they want "continuous improvement"; they seek "optimal performance"; and they often demand "perfection" from their people.

In my role as a consultant advisor, counselor, and coach, I seek to help managers transform their concepts of productivity and success. I encourage them to concentrate on, as Jonas Salk once said, the "human value of the dollar and not the dollar value of the human."

Poetry from many sources sustains me and keeps me centered, because poetry requires that I look for the meaning beneath the words—that I abandon the obvious and read with a consciousness that is more meditative and reflective. Mary Oliver's poem "The Ponds" illuminates that mysterious and powerful notion that there is something greater than our human concepts of success and failure, abled and disabled, what is excellent and just plain OK. This poem helps me face the daily skepticism and convey my message to those leaders I work with that the most important, and indeed the most useful and inspiring, measurement of accomplishment is not reflected in numbers but in the satisfaction, fulfillment, and spiritual rewards of a job well done. It reminds me of one abiding truth: life and work are not about perfection.

—James A. Autry

James A. Autry, a former Fortune 500 executive, is an author, poet, and consultant whose work has significant influence on leadership thinking. Before retiring to pursue his present career, he was senior vice president at the Meredith Corporation and president of its Magazine Group. Autry has worked with disability rights groups for thirty years.

The Ponds

Every year
the lilies
are so perfect
I can hardly believe

their lapped light crowding
the black,
mid-summer ponds.
Nobody could count all of them—

the muskrats swimming
among the pads and the grasses
can reach out
their muscular arms and touch

only so many, they are that
rife and wild.
But what in this world
is perfect?

I bend closer and see
how this one is clearly lopsided—
and that one wears an orange blight—
and this one is a glossy cheek

half nibbled away—
and that one is a slumped purse
full of its own
unstoppable decay.

Still, what I want in my life
is to be willing
to be dazzled—
to cast aside the weight of facts

and maybe even
to float a little
above this difficult world.
I want to believe I am looking

into the white fire of a great mystery.
I want to believe that the imperfections are
    nothing—
that the light is everything—that it is more
    than the sum
of each flawed blossom rising and fading.
    And I do.

—*Mary Oliver*

Winning is the broadly accepted goal of political work. Yet there is a substantial chance that all your sweat and passion will amount to nothing and be swept away once the election is over. At least it feels that way when you lose.

I have come to understand that this is a shallow view. In fact, engaging passionately in electoral politics has a spiritual parallel to the Buddhist monks who spend weeks creating beautiful intricate mandalas with colored sand. They fully invest themselves in the collaborative creation of art, which will be blown or swept away soon after it is completed.

While putting heart and soul into supporting an ideal may lead to heartbreak, it is a noble act. Giving yourself to a vision of a better world nourishes the spirit, and building community around shared ideals makes the community richer.

But I still have to come to terms with the losses associated with the work that I do. At these times, I can think of few things more renewing and sustaining than sitting with my daughter on my lap reading from our poetry book: Wallace Stevens's poem alongside Wrabe Aska's beautiful and whimsical image of children and fish aloft above a vibrant spring landscape—a world where dreams and beauty are merged, and everything is possible.

The loss of an election may sadden us, but it does not end our work. The clouds still fly round and we must continue to work for peace, for justice, and the health of the planet.

—*Joan Blades*

Joan Blades is cofounder of MoveOn.org and MomsRising.org; she is also a contributing blogger to the *Huffington Post.* Blades is a software entrepreneur, nature lover, former attorney-mediator, coauthor of *The Motherhood Manifesto,* author of *Mediate Your Divorce,* artist, Sunday soccer player, mother, and a true believer in the power of the grassroots.

When I became chairman and CEO of the largest investor-owned electric utility in Indiana in 1988, I faced diverging roads. The first, more traveled, road admitted only corporate executives and shareholders. It was marked by shifting expectations and gyrating quarterly profits. The second road was wilder, not clearly marked; here I saw the competing needs of many different stakeholders.

I chose the latter road. Not only would I care about investors and work to earn them a fair return, but I also would focus on customers, employees, policymakers, regulators, suppliers, partners, communities, the environment, and the future generation. To get there, I sat down with my colleagues; we listened to our stakeholders to figure out how we could balance their competing wants and needs. It takes more time and it's not easy, but in the end we get better results and can contend with threats like climate change.

This road less traveled has been my "true north," and following it has helped my leadership team through good times and bad. "Knowing how way leads onto way," I realize that this holistic approach to stakeholder stewardship has been missing from corporate governance.

Before my Indiana appointment, I worked briefly at Enron in its early days. Had that company chosen such a road of stewardship instead of hubris, would it have fallen? I think not.

Caring about all stakeholders is not easy, nor is it popular with all investors, but the holistic approach is the basis for real corporate governance and sustainability.

—James E. Rogers

James E. Rogers is chairman, president, and CEO of Duke Energy Corporation. Before the merger of Duke Energy and Cinergy Corp. in 2006, Rogers served as Cinergy chairman and CEO for more than eleven years. He has also been a federal energy regulator, state public consumer advocate, trial attorney, and journalist.

The Road Not Taken

Two roads diverged in a yellow wood,
And sorry I could not travel both
And be one traveler, long I stood
And looked down one as far as I could
To where it bent in the undergrowth;

Then took the other, as just as fair,
And having perhaps the better claim,
Because it was grassy and wanted wear;
Though as for that the passing there
Had worn them really about the same,

And both that morning equally lay
In leaves no step had trodden black.
Oh, I kept the first for another day!
Yet knowing how way leads on to way,
I doubted if I should ever come back.

I shall be telling this with a sigh
Somewhere ages and ages hence:
Two roads diverged in a wood, and I—
I took the one less traveled by,
And that has made all the difference.

—Robert Frost

Kids are riddles: mysterious, full of hidden possibilities, always "more than meets the eye." Each child is unique, each a bundle of talents, limitations, and aspirations; their identities are fluid.

All kids should be seen in such a way. A proper educational system would look into every child's mysteries and possibilities and then work out each "riddle." I work as a teacher in a special one-year program designed to help students from Boston with big promise but with few resources, who have finished the eighth grade, make it into the top competitive public and private high schools. My colleagues and I believe in the "star charts on the inner walls" of these students and work to help them become strong, thoughtful, broad-minded scholars.

I continually remind myself to empathize, to keep an open mind, to live with them in the world of childhood, not to be impatient, not to jump to conclusions. The virtues within this poem—curiosity, sensitivity, fanciful imagination—are essential to teaching and leadership.

The spirit of this wonderful poem reminds me, too, of how important humor and a light-hearted approach are when I'm working or playing with kids. The world is increasingly serious for kids: adult concerns intrude; fancy is squeezed out by practicality and utility. Kids should have as much "perhaps" and "as though" as possible; they should be encouraged to dream; they should imagine, and they should smile.

—Dean Conway

Dean Conway began working as an English teacher and a soccer coach in 1973. Since then, he has worked as the state coach and director of coaching for the Massachusetts Youth Soccer Association and has taught at four schools. He now teaches and coaches at Beacon Academy in Boston.

Stone

Go inside a stone.
That would be my way.
Let somebody else become a dove
Or gnash with a tiger's tooth.
I am happy to be a stone.

From the outside the stone is a riddle:
No one knows how to answer it.
Yet within, it must be cool and quiet
Even though a cow steps on it full weight,
Even though a child throws it in a river;
The stone sinks, slow, unperturbed
To the river bottom
Where the fishes come to knock on it
And listen.

I have seen sparks fly out
When two stones are rubbed,
So perhaps it is not dark inside after all;
Perhaps there is a moon shining
From somewhere, as though behind a hill—
Just enough light to make out
The strange writings, the star-charts
On the inner walls.

—Charles Simic

As a pastor, Monday mornings were the worst. I wish I could say that I was—and am—spiritually mature enough that no matter how the sermon went, no matter how many people came to church, no matter what the offering was, my mood was always the same. I wish I could say that, but I cannot. Like most people, I want to do well and make a difference in the world through my work.

The tricky part is that more often than not, the results of our efforts are not visible. We want to do well, but what does that mean? What does "well" look like? You may think that as a pastor I would be immune to our culture's obsession with quick results, measurable, show-me-the-bottom-line, tangible proof kind of success, but I am not. The ups and downs of all these Sunday morning variables affected my Monday morning mood.

I learned to seek solace from the "Monday morning funk" through this poem by Wendell Berry. Berry's words help me return to the truth that so often my best efforts must be done and "left to grace." And reminds me that for a pastor, or anyone else who seeks to do good work, the mood she or he should experience most often is a "Sabbath mood," a mood resulting from a deep sense of knowing that no matter what the immediate visible, tangible, measurable "results" may be, God is at work in the world.

—*Jay F. Smith*

Jay F. Smith is district superintendent of the Madisonville district of the Kentucky Annual Conference of the United Methodist Church. Jay is a native of Kentucky and lives in Madisonville with his wife, Marian, and his twelve-year-old son, Jericho. He enjoys reading, being outdoors, and playing golf with his son.

Sabbaths

Whatever is foreseen in joy
Must be lived out from day to day.
Vision held open in the dark
By our ten thousand days of work.
Harvest will fill the barn; for that
The hand must ache, the face must sweat.

And yet no leaf or grain is filled
By work of ours; the field is tilled
And left to grace. That we may reap,
Great work is done while we're asleep.

When we work well, a Sabbath mood
Rests on our day, and finds it good.

—Wendell Berry

In my third year of medical school, at the peak of my belief in the unquestionable omniscience and beneficence of medicine, I was told by a professor that the first item on any problem list should always be Inadequate Database. I tried to see this as a way of saying, "the more we know, the more we can help." I also tried to frame it as a way that the sometimes-arrogant face of medicine could be humble and self-effacing: "We will never know enough; please forgive us and bear with us as we try harder." But still, something about the dictum that suggested that we were on a relentless search for data troubled me.

I am not a foe of evidence-based medicine, nor will I ever propose that soothsayers be invited into the American Medical Association. I am the father of two children with kidney transplants, so, in a sense, their lives are in debt to "the process of finding out."

The human genome project, genetic splicing, stem cell research, and numerous other frontiers of medicine are all deep and complicated realms of knowledge. Auden acknowledges our intuitive sense of loss, a dark side, involved in acquiring and using this knowledge. In "the process of finding out," we must ask and answer equally complicated and deep questions about "what we wanted the knowledge for." The answer cannot be "for an adequate database." And we must also realize that, although we are able to change the world, it may not be for the better.

—*Eric Walsh, M.D.*

Eric Walsh, M.D., as a young man joined a band and worked in the
cardiology department of George Washington Hospital.
He found it so powerful he went to night school so he could apply to
medical school. He is associate chairman of Family Medicine at
Beth Israel Hospital and still plays guitar professionally.

After Reading a Child's Guide to Modern Physics

If all a top physicist knows
About the Truth be true,
Then, for all the so-and so's,
Futility and grime,
Our common world contains,
We have a better time
Than the Greater Nebulae do,
Or the atoms in our brains.

Marriage is rarely bliss
But, surely, it would be worse
As particles to pelt
At thousands of miles per sec
About a universe
In which a lover's kiss
Would either not be felt
Or break the loved one's neck.

Though the face at which I stare
While shaving it be cruel
For year after year, it repels
An ageing suitor, it has,
Thank God, sufficient mass
To be altogether there,
Not an indeterminate gruel
Which is partly somewhere else.

Our eyes prefer to suppose
That a habitable place
Has a geocentric view,
That architects enclose
A quiet euclidian space:
Exploded myths—but who
Would feel at home a-straddle
An ever expanding saddle?

This passion of our kind
For the process of finding out
Is a fact one can hardly doubt,
But I would rejoice in it more
If I knew more clearly what
We wanted the knowledge for,
Felt certain still that the mind
Is free to know or not.

It has chosen once, it seems,
And whether our concern
For magnitude's extremes
Really become a creature
Who comes in a median size,
Or politicizing Nature
Be altogether wise
Is something we shall learn.

—*W. H. Auden*

As this poem makes refreshingly clear, leadership is relative. The poet is a leader in his field; an accomplished college professor, renowned biographer of major poets, and author of six volumes of poetry. But his status is no match for eighteen kindergarteners. His wife, Eileen, also a teacher, clearly is the expert leader here.

I knew early in life that I wanted to make a difference for children. I became a teacher-principal. I helped develop a national elementary education model. I wrote books and gave workshops and became a respected leader in my field. But I grew further away from the children. I gradually realized that the teacher I was meant to be had become an uncomfortable leader.

What a remarkable journey we take to rediscover our gifts and authentic calling. There are many paths we take that seem so right at the time we take them, that turn out to be mistaken. I am a teacher who is meant to be with children. I found out that making a difference does not mean following the path to the top of your field. In fact, that may be a place of loss and loneliness once you get there.

Now, late in my career, I have returned to being a public elementary school principal and a teacher of educators in small group settings. I am back home where the children and teachers in my school as well as my own grandchildren teach me every day who I am. I feed on their every word.

—*Robert (Chip) Wood*

Robert (Chip) Wood has been working with children in one capacity or another since 1960. He is author of *Yardsticks: Children in the Classroom, Ages 4–14* and other educational books and articles. He is cofounder of The Responsive Classroom approach to elementary education. He is currently principal of Sheffield School in Montague, Massachusetts.

The Peaceable Kingdom

Once my wife brought home (I swear)
eighteen five-year-olds. Eighteen,
her entire kindergarten class.
I say eighteen, though I have no certain

proof that was the number, other
than eighteen was what Eileen,
my wife, told me was the number
who'd been there. The kids themselves, I mean,

never stood still long enough
for me to make a count.
I remember meeting them (en masse)
as I watched them all suddenly mount

the back porch two by two, the other
teacher and three mothers bringing up
the rear. The kids seemed orderly enough,
but as the first one reached the top

of the porch steps, I could feel
their little engines already beginning to shake
the joists and beams around me.
Eileen & the big ones went inside, to make

sure the chocolate milk & cookies
were all done. I was to hold the fort
alone for the next five minutes, talk
to them, introduce myself, hold court,

sort of maintain order, you understand?
For maybe three, four seconds the line
kept order, an order tighter, friends,
than what you may be hearing here in mine,

and then (like that) the whole thing fell apart.
The baby falcons could not hear
the falconer, the great invisible clockwork
spring that held it all together

suddenly went *boing!* as first one
then two then all eighteen were rolling head
over heels somersaulting down the hill
behind the house. They demanded to be fed.

They grew fangs & talons. They went
bouncing off the walls. Their groans & shouts increased.
Except as an old peartree up which to climb
or something to get round, I had already ceased

even to exist, and I was screaming
for Eileen. In a moment she was there,
and the unsprung revolutionary mass
returned instantly to order, pair by pair by pair,

with hot chocolate & a cookie for each kid.
Friends, I saw her take that lilliputian horde
& read them all a story. I saw them flock around her,
I saw them feeding on her every word.

—*Paul Mariani*

I came across this poem when I was a young girl, wondering what it meant to be "truly great." I thought my parents were "truly great," but I knew their names would never appear in history books. Gradually, I began to understand that "greatness" and "fame" are not the same thing. Greatness is an inner quality, connected to the way leaders are being, not just to what they are doing. The truly great are characterized by honor, delight, a passionate heart, and the ambition "in their lives" to fight for life.

There are two lines in this poem that pull me up short when I become too immersed in the thousand-and-one emergencies of decision making:

> Never to allow gradually the traffic to smother
> With noise and fog, the flowering of the spirit.

I attempt to remember, every day, that leadership is not about the "traffic" but about encouraging the flowering of spirit in those whose lives I touch. Sometimes this means paying extra attention to a project or an idea that an employee has generated. And sometimes this means creating what I call "systems of remembrance and appreciation,"—such as arranging individual "birthday conversations" with each employee every year.

I think of those whose lives touched mine with delight and honor and a passionate heart. Their names may not be remembered except by the "waving grass," the clouds, the wind, and me. But I am grateful.

—*Betty Sue Flowers*

Betty Sue Flowers is director of the Lyndon Baines Johnson Presidential Library and Museum. Previously, she was Kelleher Professor of English and a member of the Distinguished Teachers Academy at the University of Texas at Austin. She is a poet, an editor, and a business consultant, with many publications, including *Joseph Campbell and the Power of Myth.*

The Truly Great

I think continually of those who were truly great.
Who, from the womb, remembered the soul's history
Through corridors of light, where the hours are suns,
Endless and singing. Whose lovely ambition
Was that their lips, still touched with fire,
Should tell of the Spirit clothed from head to foot in song.
And who hoarded from the Spring branches
The desires falling across their bodies like blossoms.

What is precious is never to forget
The essential delight of the blood drawn from ageless springs
Breaking through rocks in worlds before our earth.
Never to deny its pleasure in the morning simple light
Nor its grave evening demand for love.
Never to allow gradually the traffic to smother
With noise and fog, the flowering of the spirit.

Near the snow, near the sun, in the highest fields,
See how these names are fêted by the waving grass
And by the streamers of white cloud
And whispers of wind in the listening sky.
The names of those who in their lives fought for life,
Who wore at their hearts the fire's centre.
Born of the sun, they traveled a short while towards the sun
And left the vivid air signed with their honour.

—Stephen Spender

I used to be a Wall Street dealmaker. As an investment banker, I investigated the financial health of companies, deciphered their earnings reports, and sorted through executive communications that increasingly confused and misled investors, employees, and customers. Finally, I had enough. Twelve years ago, I pioneered a process that measures CEO candor and shows how this is linked to higher stock prices. With such a prize, I wonder why so many CEOs still use motivation-killing clichés like "leverage our strengths" and "bright future ahead."

Confounded by this triumph of fog over truth and even profit, I remember my grandmother Cora. During the heyday of Spam and processed cheese, she made me eat whole grains and organic vegetables. My friends thought our meals were hilarious. But who's laughing now? The once radical notion that "we are what we eat" has transformed the practice of medicine, and it has spawned a multi-billion-dollar health food industry.

I encourage my business clients to adopt a similar philosophy: "we become what we write, what we say." Some folks find it frightening to own the creative power of their words. But leaders who authentically and truthfully communicate are more successful, in the long term, than those who rely on spin. Great leaders shed light into dark places rather than intentionally fabricating shadows and smog. Tagore's poem and my grandmother's steadfastness remind me that I am not alone. I only have to look for support—and invite it in.

—L. J. Rittenhouse

L. J. Rittenhouse is president of andBEYOND Communications, a consulting company that benchmarks CEO candor. She advises corporate leaders on the financial benefits of capital stewardship and clear communication. A former investment banker, she wrote *Do Business With People You Can Tru$t* and is a founding member of Families with Children from China.

The Grasp of Your Hand

Let me not pray to be sheltered from dangers,
but to be fearless in facing them.

Let me not beg for the stilling of my pain, but
for the heart to conquer it.

Let me not crave in anxious fear to be saved,
but hope for the patience to win my freedom.

Grant me that I may not be a coward, feeling
Your mercy in my success alone; but let me find
the grasp of Your hand in my failure.

—Rabindranath Tagore

My passion for creating better health care lives in ordinary routines, like last Friday:

RESIDENT M.D.: I'm stuck. [The survey that he had administrated indicated that only a small percentage of cancer patients had arranged for a formal advance directive about care and life support, and he wanted to develop an action path to improve that situation.]

ME: What helped those who have made a plan? [I thought their experience might help.]

RESIDENT: I don't know. [It was safe; learning may be just ahead.]

ME: Could you ask them? [The questions, the analysis, and the creative changes to the systems were emerging. A teacher's humble flashback: the resident had done well in my class that had introduced but obviously not covered the topic!]

RESIDENT: Sure. [A quiet smile—a journal note.]

Because good patient care accompanies good learning, we encourage physicians-in-training to immerse themselves in the grace of the real world as they develop their practical wisdom—meeting particular people, addressing particular needs. Their learning connects living and dying. We remind them that patients are worried, sick people, often not at their best but trying to be civil. We expect that these doctors-to-be will become "glue" for the cracks in broken systems. We encourage them to be aware of the love underneath their caregiving and its reciprocal effect on them.

This is all about being present and attentive, being creative, and keeping the fire. Why should this be so hard to learn? Sometimes it makes me tired, frustrated, and even privately grouchy. Then this poem reminds me of what I, too, have learned so far.

—Paul Batalden, M.D.

Paul Batalden, M.D., is professor of pediatrics, Community and Family Medicine, at Dartmouth Medical School. He teaches quality measurement and improvement in the Center for the Evaluative Clinical Sciences and directs the graduate medical program for leadership development. He is a pediatrician and has been a teacher-physician for thirty-nine years.

What I Have Learned So Far

Meditation is old and honorable, so why should I not sit, every morning of my life, on the hillside, looking into the shining world? Because, properly attended to, delight, as well as havoc, is suggestion. Can one be passionate about the just, the ideal, the sublime, and the holy, and yet commit to no labor in its cause? I don't think so.

All summations have a beginning, all effect has a story, all kindness begins with the sown seed. Thought buds toward radiance. The gospel of light is the crossroads of—indolence, or action.

Be ignited, or be gone.

—*Mary Oliver*

When I first found this poem, I had to memorize it. When I learned the poem, I had to share it. When I began to share it, I couldn't stop. I shared it with unsuspecting audiences at birthday parties, dinner parties, book clubs; for friends on walks, for colleagues at conferences; to introduce a former secretary of labor; at staff meetings and board retreats, at Passover Seders; in South Africa for 350 first-generation college students; for my wife-to-be on our first dinner date.

This is my "just add humans" poem, but there are limits. It only seems to appeal to people with bodies, especially those of us who use our bodies to work during the day and then sleep in these bodies at night.

At the Kellogg Foundation, we swing our sickles made of money through the tall grass of civics every day—heady and potentially precarious work if the mind's engineering is not leavened by the heart's compassion, the soul's singing, and the conscience's wary concerns. And this is our work, our challenge to catch and cultivate all the voices inside us just as we seek to find partners who surely hear their own voices calling them as we work together in the fields of philanthropy.

Imagine my fearful and mischievous joy one evening at a conference to be offered a seat next to Billy Collins at dinner before the reading. Be still my heart; please don't spill that warm milk, but how could I—or one of me—not ask him, do you take requests?

—Sterling K. Speirn

Sterling K. Speirn is president and CEO of the W. K. Kellogg Foundation in Battle Creek, Michigan. Before his previous philanthropic experience at Apple Computer and the Peninsula Community Foundation, he worked as a school teacher, an attorney, and a community health administrator.

The Night House

Every day the body works in the fields of the world
mending a stone wall
or swinging a sickle through the tall grass—
the grass of civics, the grass of money—
and every night the body curls around itself
and listens for the soft bells of sleep.

But the heart is restless and rises
from the body in the middle of the night,
leaves the trapezoidal bedroom
with its thick, pictureless walls
to sit by herself at the kitchen table
and heat some milk in a pan.

And the mind gets up too, puts on a robe
and goes downstairs, lights a cigarette,
and opens a book on engineering.
Even the conscience awakens
and roams from room to room in the dark,
darting away from every mirror like a strange fish.

And the soul is up on the roof
in her nightdress, straddling the ridge,
singing a song about the wildness of the sea
until the first rip of pink appears in the sky.
Then, they all will return to the sleeping body
the way a flock of birds settles back into a tree,

resuming their daily colloquy,
talking to each other or themselves
even through the heat of the long afternoons.
Which is why the body—the house of voices—
sometimes puts down its metal tongs, its needle, or its pen
to stare into the distance,

to listen to all its names being called
before bending again to its labor.

—*Billy Collins*

Dare to Endure

$\mathcal{L}$ eaders live in the gap between what should be and what is. That is where the work that most needs doing resides. On one side of the gap, our dreams, our aspirations, our best hopes for each other and our communities call to us. The other side is the world as we know it: beset with human frailty, strife, and pent-up hope. It is here amidst complex and competing forces that pull and yank on their time and beliefs that leaders do their work. It takes guts to set forth and endure life in this gap; there is no golden bullet or magic fix.

We can hope, as Seamus Heaney tells us, for "miracles and cures and healing wells" but the real work takes time and courageous endurance. Jack Gilbert reminds us that "the abnormal is not courage." There is no quick fix or "amazed understanding," leadership is about endurance and "the beauty/that is of many days. Steady and clear./It is the normal excellence, of long accomplishment."

The stories and commentaries in this section tell of leaders who work day-after-day on a cumulative quest. They tell us of striving to foster interfaith healing after 9/11, of standing up by telling their story about sexual abuse, of protecting the natural world. They recognize that they must step into the fray but also must have great patience, as change is slow. They must be like "drops of water falling on the stone."

I can still picture where I first read this line of Browning's poem. I heard it as a challenge to learn and understand foreign languages and cultures. I began with Latin and Spanish; I mowed lawns in exchange for Russian.

Languages were keys to a world I wanted to reach, a world I wanted to serve. I chose a career embedded in languages—the Foreign Service—and sought assignments only to places where I knew the language.

I served as ambassador to Romania, India, and Chile. An American ambassador can attract a great deal of attention, especially if able to use the language of the country. Even in the dictatorships of Ceausescu's Romania and Pinochet's Chile, I had access to people striving to have their rights acknowledged and respected.

In Romania, a dissident historian gave me a manuscript to read, for which he was later imprisoned. I refused the authorities' demand to return the manuscript until my friend was released. That incident contributed to, for a time at least, a more open atmosphere in Romania. In Chile, I used the formal public occasion of presenting my credentials to Pinochet to stress that the ills of democracy are best cured by more democracy. That statement and my subsequent, very visible emphasis on human rights clearly aligned the United States with the struggle for an early return to democracy in Chile.

Human rights remain both a dream and a battle. Grasped today, they may slip away tomorrow. God help us if we don't keep reaching out beyond our grasp.

—*Harry Barnes*

Harry Barnes served as director general of the Foreign Service and director of personnel, as well as ambassador to Romania, India, and Chile. As a career foreign service officer, he is currently helping organize projects involving Indian, Pakistani, and American scientists in geology and agrobiotechnology and is a senior advisor to the Asia Society.

"Oh, my friend" is a poem for bridge builders—in the inner world and the outer. It invites us, abiding in the loving essence of our Provider, to discover our true selves and dwell in peace with others. It has inspired me to devote my life to building bridges of interfaith understanding around the world.

Building bridges is demanding, delicate work. We work with outwardly competing, hostile traditions yet create safe space. In Berlin, we convened Jews, Christians, and Muslims from the Middle East. They divided into groups of three to encounter the other. In one trio was a Jewish woman whose son was nearly killed by a suicide bomber, a young Muslim woman who had never spoken with a Jew, and a Roman Catholic woman from Argentina—three islands in an ocean of uneasiness.

We asked, "Please share the greatest gift you have received from your religion. Please share your vision of the world as you would like it to be." As they spoke and listened, bridges of understanding, affection, and shared commitment connected the islands. Three strangers became three sisters, each committed to return home and work to build a better world with others of different faiths.

This work in the outer world is made possible by the inner work that connects us with our Source. Coming to know ourselves as children of one Provider and citizens of Earth, we become a global community from every continent, culture, and faith, sharing the sacred and serving the world.

—*Charles Gibbs*

Charles Gibbs is the executive director of the United Religions Initiative (URI), which was founded in 2000 and is committed to promoting enduring, daily interfaith cooperation and ending religiously motivated violence. The URI includes thousands of members in over fifty countries representing more than one hundred religions, spiritual expressions, and indigenous traditions.

Oh, my friend

Oh, my friend:
Love makes the world of creation a
    possibility
and the ecstasy of ascension a will.
Look around yourself and see a universe
saturated by the fragrance of love.

If there was no love and the endurance for
such longing, then who could
    beautify words
into majestic melodies?

If there was no breeze to gracefully
    caress the
hair of the beloved, then how could
    the lover
see the revealing face of the beloved?
Such longing is to gracefully return to the
Provider, in the state of perfection.

Oh, my friend:
do not become a slave of worship, but
understand the meaning of worship;
understand the meaning of Divine, Allah,
and practice to be pious and peaceful;
become a true human being, as becoming a
true human being is the key to salvation.

Oh, my friend:
if you have chosen an inner path,
    remember
that we all are travelers, our moments are
passing and we are passing with them.

Your wealth will not remain forever
    and your
pain will not last, so do not become a
    slave to
your wealth nor to your pain.

If you are a person of an inner path,
    then you
are a person of peace, so make peace with
yourself and your surroundings.

—*Ezzeddin Nasafi*

At twenty-two I went to Tunisia to start a school for disabled kids in the back of a mosque in a small town where people believed such children could not be taught. Before I left home, a colleague gave me this poem. In the evenings I would read it as I reflected on another day spent trying to help people think in new ways about kids and education.

Through this poem, Gilbert taught me that work is all about the "normal excellence, of long accomplishment." We want something—an enemy, an opponent that we can ride out against and battle, the way the Poles rode out on horses against the German tanks. We like that image: we hear the soundtrack swelling up and see ourselves sweeping in to rescue those we were asked to save. But real leadership is not like that. The real work does not take place on stages or stallions.

In Tunisia, it took place through conversations in homes, cafés, and shops— conversations most didn't hear and actions that few saw. Today, these conversations happen in the hall of my school where I stop to talk with a student or after school talking with a colleague about the work we love and seek to better understand. Twenty-two years later, Gilbert's poem still reminds me that my work is made up of the "beauty of many days," that my accomplishment is "the thing steady and clear," which is to say my daily effort to make a difference in the classroom, the school, and the country.

—Jim Burke

Jim Burke teaches English at Burlingame High School. He was awarded the prestigious National Council of Teachers of English Intellectual Freedom Award for his contributions to the field of education. He is the author of *50 Essential Lessons: Tools and Techniques for Teaching English Language Arts* and *Letters to a New Teacher.*

The Abnormal Is Not Courage

The Poles rode out from Warsaw against the German
tanks on horses. Rode knowing, in sunlight, with sabers.
A magnitude of beauty that allows me no peace.
And yet this poem would lessen that day. Question
the bravery. Say it's not courage. Call it a passion.
Would say courage isn't that. Not at its best.
It was impossible, and with form. They rode in sunlight.
Were mangled. But I say courage is not the abnormal.
Not the marvelous act. Not Macbeth with fine speeches.
The worthless can manage in public, or for the moment.
It is too near the whore's heart: the bounty of impulse,
and the failure to sustain even small kindness.
Not the marvelous act, but the evident conclusion of being.
Not strangeness, but a leap forward of the same quality.
Accomplishment. The even loyalty. But fresh.
Not the Prodigal Son, nor Faustus. But Penelope.
The thing steady and clear. Then the crescendo.
The real form. The culmination. And the exceeding.
Not the surprise. The amazed understanding. The marriage,
not the month's rapture. Not the exception. The beauty
that is of many days. Steady and clear.
It is the normal excellence, of long accomplishment.

—Jack Gilbert

For a Muslim interfaith activist, the aftermath of 9/11 felt like a never-ending nightmare. I spent my days posting essays on the Internet and giving talks to small groups of people explaining Islam, defending America, and entreating us all to fly the flag of coexistence. My words were received politely and dismissed immediately. The peaceful, participatory pluralism I talked about sounded like a pipe dream to most people. The world was beginning to brace for war; "how soon?" and "where first?" were the big questions.

After several months of this, I began to question how much I believed in my own vision. I needed a reminder that the path of my faith—the dream of a common life together—had some basis in reality. I had read a great deal about al Andalus, a multicultural society led by generous and tolerant Muslim rulers that had flourished in southern Spain one thousand years earlier. The milieu of al Andalus inspired the astounding architecture of the al Hambra palace, the brilliant commentaries of Aristotle by the Muslim philosopher Averroes, and a burst of creativity in the Jewish community, who were held in high esteem and given protection by the emirs.

When I was walking with my wife in the old city of Cordoba, we found this poem by Ibn Arabi hanging on the wall of a Morrocan tea shop. It was exactly what I needed: poetry of possibility, poetry with prophecy, poetry like prayer.

—*Eboo Patel*

Eboo Patel is founder and executive director of the Interfaith Youth Core (www.ifyc.org), an international organization building the interfaith youth movement. He is author of *Acts of Faith: The Story of an American Muslim, the Struggle for the Soul of a Generation* and a regular blogger for the *Washington Post/Newsweek Magazine*'s "On Faith" section.

There was a time I would reject those

There was a time I would reject those
who were not of my faith.
But now, my heart has grown capable
of taking on all forms.
It is a pasture for gazelles,
An abbey for monks.
A table for the Torah,
Kaaba for the pilgrim.
My religion is love.
Whichever the route love's caravan shall take,
That shall be the path of my faith.

—Ibn Arabi

What turned me into a "green warrior"? I certainly didn't start out that way. When I first stepped up to a podium, I was so nervous that I shook. It could have been the end.

Instead I remembered that "my life was not a solitary thing." I remembered my child's laughter; I remembered the last remaining wildernesses; I remembered the crossing of oceans; I remembered the sunrises and sunsets. These images from nature awakened in me the strength, courage, and commitment to let my voice rise and work for a greener world.

Given the challenges of our time, I believe we need a worldview that shifts us toward a more positive future. I work to establish dynamic worldwide networks of people who have the capacities and skills to promote policies and programs engaged in making the world a better place. Through these networks, I strive to bring innovative solutions to restore peace and prosperity to regions around the world that have been devastated by war, ecological catastrophe, economic collapse, or significant political instability. Especially in Africa, where I once lived, I am determined to not let any of my African partners down, even though the process of getting anything done is slow and challenging.

Together, we have been creating ecovillages—in urban or rural settings—that integrate ecological design, alternative energy, and community building. Through these ecovillages, community and grassroots leaders emerge empowered and inspired by the vision and values of sustainability. Then they too begin to sing with the wind.

—Annie Goeke de La Bouillerie

Annie Goeke de La Bouillerie is a leader in the Greens and Peace movement. A worldwide and a community activist, she cofounded an international peace organization and currently codirects the Earth Rights Institute, which initiates and supports programs that address poverty through ecological community development, humanitarian aid, and earth rights policies.

Let me remember

Let

    me

        remember

beyond forgetting—

    let

        me

            remember—

         —

         —

let me remember always

    for my spirit is often shrouded in the

        mists—

let me remember beyond forgetting

    that my life is not a solitary thing—

        it is a bit of the rushing tide

a leaf of the bending tree—

    a kernel of grain in the golden wheat fields—

        a whisper of wind about the mountaintop—

a reflection of sunlight upon the

        shining waters—

it is fleeting—

        it is of the moment

    it is timeless—

        it is of eternity.

—Winston O. Abbott

When I was young, I once heard somebody say, "open your heart." I remember repeatedly asking my parents. "How can I open my heart?" They guided me to Rumi, the thirteenth-century mystic, and taught me to meditate on his poetry to illuminate verses of the Qur'an.

A primary spiritual practice, my parents explained, is to embrace not only the joys of life but also its sorrows. Don't run toward pain; just don't run away from it. Little by little, with compassion for yourself, envelop and enfold your sadness. Be present with your grief. Gently, allow your heart to break. By grace of God, you will usher in an abundance of riches within.

In 1991 both my parents died suddenly. Overwhelmed with sadness, I recalled Rumi's poem about the heart's matrix and allowed my heart to break. In the spaciousness I experienced inside my heart, I was able to astonishingly feel peace and joy.

As a Muslim Sufi minister, passionate about interfaith understanding, I work with clerics of other faiths. My heart rejoices over commonalities in our religions, but I am also mindful of differences and of my feelings of judgment and separation. But as I hold these feelings and allow them to dissolve into the spaciousness of my heart, something softens and shifts inside me. Theological differences no longer loom as large, and there is ample space for personal bonding. A ruby-like insight arises from the wellspring of my heart: it was not my religion that was bruised, but my ego.

—*Jamal Rahman*

Jamal Rahman is a Muslim Sufi minister at the Interfaith Community Church and adjunct faculty at Seattle University. He wrote *The Fragrance of Faith: The Enlightened Heart of Islam*. Rahman is passionate about interfaith work. He believes interfaith is not about conversion; it is about completion.

From "What is This Fragrance"

. . . but come! Take a pick-axe
and break apart
your stony self

the heart's matrix
is glutted with rubies
springs of laughter
are buried in your breast.

—*Rumi*

I am not a leader by nature, rather more of an observer—someone who prefers to stand on the sidelines watching others make their mark. This changed when, out of the blue, our older son, a healthy thirteen-year-old, was diagnosed with a rare brain tumor. As it was only weeks after that terrible storm hit Indonesia, taking thousands of lives, it was natural for us to relate to "tsunami" as a metaphor. This was a personal tsunami. Our former lives were swept away in a single moment, all certainties gone.

I have learned that while one is not necessarily born to lead, life can thrust leadership upon you. It's like a cosmic game of hot potato. When the music stops and you're the one left holding the ball, you have no choice. You cannot not act, so you do. You take charge. You figure out what must be done. And you throw yourself into it 100 percent, especially when you're fighting to save your child.

Over the past eighteen months, my son has faced chemotherapy and radiation treatments, surgery, and bone marrow transplants. I have led by searching for answers, challenging experts, investigating options, staring down consent forms filled with grim outcomes, and believing in my son's ability to come through. Through endless hospital nights and countless moments of near-panic, I have reflected upon this proverb. We all walk a narrow bridge. Look any direction but straight ahead and you might falter. The essential thing is to stay focused, moving forward, one step at a time.

—Jaime Banks

Jaime Banks has a background in communications research and public health campaigns, specializing in the pre-testing of cancer communications for patients, medical professionals, and the public. She found herself on the other side of the table as the primary caregiver for her teenage son, who was diagnosed with a brain tumor in 2005.

I drove to my office on Capitol Hill that September morning, thinking what a bright, clear day it was. An hour later I met with a congressman, discussing The Faith & Politics Institute's work to help members of Congress listen to what Abraham Lincoln called "the better angels of our nature." An aide interrupted and told us we had to evacuate the building. We walked out and saw the smoke rising from the Pentagon.

By sunset on September 11, 2001, questions crowded my heart and my mind. How much longer will I be alive? Where will this take us as a nation and a people? Is there a word from God in the midst of the terror, fear, and fury? For a week I wondered and wandered.

By grace, on September 19, I had an appointment with Ambassador Sheila Sisulu to discuss bringing a congressional delegation to South Africa to study the transition from apartheid and the reconciliation process in her country. As I drove up Rock Creek Parkway, this poem came to mind. The people in South Africa had suffered, had tortured one another, had gotten hurt and gotten hard. They also experienced a great sea-change on the far side of revenge. Given this, I could again believe a further shore is reachable. I could believe in miracles, in cures, in healing wells. I could believe in the capacity of political leaders to recognize—and eventually heed—the better angels of our nature. I could resume my work.

—Doug Tanner

Doug Tanner is a United Methodist minister and senior adviser to The Faith & Politics Institute in Washington, D.C. He came of age in the South during the civil rights movement, was shaped by its spirit, and has served as a political campaign consultant and congressional aide.

From "The Cure at Troy"

Human beings suffer.
They torture one another.
They get hurt and get hard.

History says, Don't hope
On this side of the grave,
But then, once in a lifetime
The longed-for tidal wave
Of justice can rise up,
And hope and history rhyme.

So hope for a great sea-change
On the far side of revenge.
Believe that a farther shore
Is reachable from here.
Believe in miracles
And cures and healing wells.

—Seamus Heaney

Beat poet Kenneth Patchen's sarcastic verse had an irresistible edge for an adolescent in the 1960s, struggling to understand the use and abuse of power. The narrator's damning compliance incited my revolt against the influence of my parish priest, a trusted mentor, who also sexually abused me.

Patchen's poem jump-started my recovery and served as a springboard to a decades-long inquiry into the ethics of leadership and, later, "followership"—what it means to be a good follower. The wisdom we glean as followers—a role we inhabit first and always—inevitably shapes how we lead. Is worthwhile followership characterized by unwavering loyalty, blind obedience—or a commitment to inspire, to question, even to overthrow the leader?

As a journalist, a child-protection social worker, an activist, and an abuse survivor, I've been an intimate witness to the failings and successes of leaders and followers of many stripes. I've learned that, at its root, abuse of power is more complex than simple stories of good and evil.

Leadership opportunities come to followers willing to heed Patchen's entreaty to speak up "in order to . . ." (protect) a village. Long ago, I reclaimed my voice, reported the abuse, and began shedding the shame that once silenced me. Speaking openly about my experiences has strengthened me and hopefully inspired other adults to take action to prevent child sexual abuse.

Despite the risk of reprisal, courageous followers act to prevent harm-forsaking silence to safeguard both the powerless victim and the errant leader, long before lives are blown "all to hell and gone."

—Peter Pollard

Peter Pollard is the public education director for Stop It Now!—an international sexual abuse prevention organization. He worked for Massachusetts' child protection agency and is now an area leader of the Survivors Network of those Abused by Priests (SNAP). His commentaries have been widely published, including on National Public Radio.

In Order to

Apply for the position (I've forgotten now for what) I had to
marry the Second Mayor's daughter by twelve noon. The order
arrived three minutes of.

I already had a wife; the Second Mayor was childless: but I did it.

Next they told me to shave off my father's beard. All right. No
matter that he'd been a eunuch, and had succumbed in early
childhood: I did it, I shaved him.

Then they told me to burn a village; next, a fair-sized town; then,
a city; a bigger city; a small, down-at-heels country; then one of
"the great powers;" then another (another, another)—In fact, they
went right on until they'd told me to burn up every man-made
thing on the face of the earth! And I did it, I burned away every
last trace, I left nothing, nothing of any kind whatever.

Then they told me to blow it all to hell and gone! And I blew it
all to hell and gone (oh, didn't I) . . .

Now, they said, put it back together again; put it all back the way
it was when you started.

Well . . . it was my turn then to tell *them* something! Shucks, I
didn't want any job that bad.

—Kenneth Patchen

As a bereavement coordinator for a children's hospital, I try to support families after the death of a child. People ask me how I can do this work.

Yeats's image of a mind still like water guides me as I work with grieving families. I must quiet myself so that the families' own pain, fears, hopes, and needs can surface. There are no words to take away the pain, especially when a child dies, but I can bear witness to their sorrow with a gentle presence. Sometimes this is the best (and only) way to support a grieving family.

When I feel overwhelmed by the grief around me, I try to focus on returning to that still, quiet center in order to renew myself and to be of service to the families in our program. In that space I let my own fears, hopes, and needs surface and remember the blessings I have received that are life-affirming for me. I also reflect on my place and connection to the greater universe, sustained by the belief that, ultimately, we are all safe in God's care.

The amazing courage of the children facing death, the daily reminders about what is truly important in life, and the parents' ability to transform their broken hearts into open hearts are precious gifts to me. And to think that someone's life might become "clearer" or "fiercer" because of my quiet presence is powerfully rewarding.

—Elizabeth A. Keene Reder

Elizabeth A. Keene Reder serves as a bereavement coordinator for Johns Hopkins Children's Center as part of the palliative care team, Harriet Lane Compassionate Care. She has worked in hospice and palliative care for the past twelve years.

From *Earth, Fire and Water*

We can make our minds so like still water
that beings gather about us that they may see,
it may be, their own images,
and so live for a moment with a clearer,
perhaps even with a fiercer life
because of our quiet.

—*William Butler Yeats*

As the first woman from Wisconsin and the first "out" lesbian in the nation elected to Congress, I am mindful of the role I play, both symbolically and substantively, in creating change. The quest for equality under the law and in practice has been a long and ongoing struggle for people of color, women, people with disabilities, lesbian, gay, bisexual, and transgendered (LGBT) Americans, among others.

The LGBT community, while more open and more accepted than ever before, still faces opposition and, sometimes, violence in the form of hate crimes; discrimination in employment, marriage, the military, and the denial of other legal rights and protections. For me, the quest for equality and justice is personal as well as political. I am frequently invited to speak to LGBT audiences seeking reassurance, both personal and political, that full equality will someday be achieved.

Every movement for social change, whether for women's suffrage, desegregation and civil rights, workers' rights, environmental protections, or full equality for LGBT Americans, has taken time and comes at a heavy price. Often the struggle seems too long, too painful, or too difficult to pursue.

In the day-to-day quest, frustration can easily overwhelm hope. These lyrics always remind me, and I use my position to remind others, that great change takes time. Just as the majestic Grand Canyon was carved away over eons by drops of water, the cumulative action of countless individuals has the same force to create dramatic and meaningful change in society.

—Tammy Baldwin

Tammy Baldwin was first elected as representative from Wisconsin's 2nd congressional district in 1998 at age thirty-seven. She is recognized nationally for empowering young people to participate in the political process and as an advocate for universal health care, civil rights, and for those whose voices, too often, are not heard.

From "The Rock Will Wear Away"

Can we be like drops of water falling on the stone
Splashing, breaking, disbursing in air
Weaker than the stone by far but be aware
That as time goes by the rock will wear away
And the water comes again

—*Holly Near*

Leading Together

In a world that the poet Louis MacNeice describes as "incorrigibly plural," that is "crazier and more of than we think," leaders understand that going solo and operating by command and control can't resolve the complex problems of our time. We need leaders who build alliances, cultivate trust, and create conditions where diverse people can come together to do their best and most inspired work. Leadership—our contributors tell us—is about communities learning to put their collective shoulders to the wheel.

Our contributors disavow notions of the charismatic, go-it-alone paradigm buster for the idea of leader-as-community-and-bridge-builder. The real work of leadership—they tell us—is to build collaborative energy, where men and women can gather their collective voice and stand "shoulder to shoulder." They describe the leadership of listening, of question asking, of discerning the plural voices, and helping groups move forward with shared energy.

Martin Buber tells us that in the "end it is all about relationship." For those who follow, this is true.

Leadership tries its little heart out to be rational. It is forever looking for strategies, methods—any logical way to ensure success, anything that will justify its position at the head of the table.

My experience (and I'm not about to universalize this) is that the world expects a decent amount of reason in their leaders but not too much. The real issue here is messier than that, less predictable, less logical: "Does this cat care about ME? And how much?" That's what we all really want to know before we agree to follow.

And that's why every great Chief has a little shaman in him or her.

—Dan Wieden

Dan Wieden bought a beret in 1962, then started smoking and
writing horrible, horrible poetry. He wanted to be Robert Creeley.
That proved impossible so he started an ad agency,
Wieden + Kennedy, which, oddly enough, became quite successful.

The Warning

For love—I would
split open your head and put
a candle in
behind the eyes.

Love is dead in us
if we forget
the virtues of an amulet
and quick surprise.

—Robert Creeley

"What does this organization think about the role of race in violence?" This was the first question posed to me as the newly hired executive director of a national violence-prevention program. My heart simultaneously soared and sank. I immediately understood the question not to be about race but about social justice.

My conflicting emotions arose from a lifelong internal battle. Social justice had long been my quest. As a child I had wanted to be president—the one I thought could right all wrongs and make an America "where every person is free." Over the years, I recognized that who I was wasn't a president; it wasn't in my personality. I learned that I was most effective working in the background for social justice and came to see the desire to be up-front as a vanity. Yet here I was, being called out in a public meeting to provide leadership on one of the most volatile issues in our country's history. But I knew it was not for me to answer and instead punted the question back to the community members at the meeting.

I have learned through my trials in life that difficult moments serve a purpose. Life leads us to where we should be, despite our ferocious struggles against it. At the Institute for Community Peace, I work with communities that want to do more than end violence; they want America to be America. They know how this can be done—my role is to invite the questions, listen, hear, and sing their wisdom.

—Linda K. Bowen

Linda K. Bowen has served as executive director of the Institute for Community Peace (ICP) since 1995. She has over twenty-five years of experience in violence prevention, program management and development, policy analysis, research, and community building.

From "Let America Be America Again"

Let America be America again,
Let it be the dream it used to be.
Let it be the pioneer on the plain
Seeking a home where he himself is free.

(America never was America to me.) . . .

O, let my land be a land where Liberty
Is crowned with no false patriotic wreath,
But opportunity is real, and life is free,
Equality is in the air we breathe. . . .

O, let America be America again—
The land that never has been yet—
And yet must be—the land where
   every man is free. . . .

O, yes,
I say it plain,
America never was America to me,
And yet I swear this oath—
America will be! . . .

We, the people, must redeem
The land, the mines, the plants, the rivers.
The mountains and the endless plain—
All, all the stretch of these great green states—
And make America again!

—*Langston Hughes*

From "Yet Do I Marvel"

Yet do I marvel at this curious thing—
To make a poet black and bid him sing.

—*Countee Cullen*

When I was eight, I discovered the joys of the "open road" on the aqueduct, a glorious dirt path that connected all the New York river towns together. I would ride my bike for hours, totally lost in thought. I must have ridden a thousand miles, back and forth. I loved feeling so free. As Whitman writes, "From this hour, freedom! From this hour I ordain myself loos'd of limits and imaginary lines,/going where I list, my own master, total and absolute."

This experience allowed me to fearlessly embrace the open road later on in my life and career. After fourteen years with Goldman Sachs, I set off in a new direction. I launched my own asset management firm and founded 85 Broads— a comentoring, global network of over fifteen thousand visionary women.

I have challenged these women to push through real and imagined barriers that might prevent them from going boldly forward. I want them to hear Whitman and say to themselves, "I am larger, better than I thought,/I did not know I held so much goodness."

My passion is to build a community where women can be inspired by the success of each other, to stand shoulder to shoulder when times are tough, and to believe and trust in each other's goodness, integrity, and vision. To remember, "You have done such good to me,/I would do the same to you."

I have learned how to experience the joy of giving without limits or imaginary lines and to fearlessly embrace the open road.

—Janet Tiebout Hanson

Janet Tiebout Hanson is a graduate of Wheaton College and Columbia Business School. Hanson spent fourteen years at Goldman Sachs before launching Milestone Capital with her husband, Jeff. She is the founder of 85 Broads, an independent global network that inspires, empowers, and connects over seventeen thousand women worldwide.

From "Song of the Open Road"

Afoot and light-hearted I take to the open road,
Healthy, free, the world before me,
The long brown path before me, leading wherever I choose.

Henceforth I ask not good-fortune, I myself am good fortune,
Henceforth I whimper no more, postpone no more, need nothing,
Done with indoor complaints, libraries, querulous criticisms,
Strong and content, I travel the open road. . . .

O public road! I say back I am not afraid to leave you, yet I love you,
You express me better than I can express myself,
You shall be more to me than my poem.

I think heroic deeds were all conceiv'd in the open air, and all free
     poems also,
I think I could stop here myself and do miracles,
I think whatever I shall meet on the road I shall like, and whoever beholds
     me shall like me,
I think whoever I see must be happy.

From this hour I ordain myself loos'd of limits and imaginary lines,
Going where I list, my own master total and absolute,
Listening to others, considering well what they say,
Pausing, searching, receiving, contemplating,
Gently, but with undeniable will, divesting myself of the holds that would
     hold me.

I inhale great draughts of space,
The east and the west are mine, and the north and the south are mine.

I am larger, better than I thought,
I did not know I held so much goodness.

All seems beautiful to me,
I can repeat over to men and women You have done such good to me
    I would do the same to you,
I will recruit for myself and you as I go,
I will scatter myself among men and women as I go,
I will toss a new gladness and roughness among them,
Whoever denies me, it shall not trouble me,
Whoever accepts me he or she shall be blessed and shall bless me.

Now if a thousand perfect men were to appear, it would not amaze me,
Now if a thousand beautiful forms of women appear'd
    it would not astonish me.

Now I see the secret of the making of the best persons,
It is to grow in the open air and to eat and sleep with the earth.

Here a great personal deed has room,
(Such a deed seizes upon the hearts of the whole race of men,
Its effusion of strength and will overwhelms law and mocks all authority and
    all argument against it.) . . .

Allons! the road is before us!
It is safe—I have tried it—my own feet have tried it well—be not detain'd!
Let the paper remain on the desk unwritten, and the book on the shelf
    unopen'd!
Let the tools remain in the workshop! let the money remain unearn'd!
Let the school stand! mind not the cry of the teacher!
Let the preacher preach in his pulpit! let the lawyer plead in the court, and
    the judge expound the law.

Camerado, I give you my hand!
I give you my love more precious than money,
I give you myself before preaching or law;
Will you give me yourself? will you come travel with me?
Shall we stick by each other as long as we live?

—*Walt Whitman*

"I'm going to have surgery next week and may not make it. I don't hold much with church, but would you do my funeral? And tell them I wasn't such a bad fella?"

I consider requests like this one from a commercial fisherman I know to be a great honor. At these moments, my work as an Episcopal priest, writer, commercial fisher, and community activist intertwine. Living and working in a small rural fishing community gives me deep access and insight into the people I serve. I experience the same hazards of fishing in open water, scarcity of fish, and low prices.

As a leader, I focus on listening to community members share their experiences and concerns. From this listening, I strive to pull together solutions to problems that at first may seem intractable. Sometimes this entails developing support for families suffering from declining fisheries, attending hearings to advocate on behalf of the fishing community, or creating a summation that honors a person's life. As a priest, I have embraced the role of servant leader, which takes on flesh in these memorial services, in working with these families, in attending these hearings.

"Snow" is a reminder that things may appear "various," "collateral and incompatible," but through careful listening there may be a bigger picture that will come into view, an action to take, a way to serve. Or a poem.

—*Irene Martin*

Irene Martin has been a writer for over thirty years and an Episcopal priest for fourteen years. She has fished commercially for salmon in Washington and Alaska. Her books include *Legacy and Testament: The Story of Columbia River Gillnetters* and *Sea Fire: Tales of Jesus and Fishing*.

Snow

The room was suddenly rich, and the great bay window was
Spawning snow and pink roses against it
Soundlessly collateral and incompatible:
World is suddener than we fancy it.

World is crazier and more of it than we think,
Incorrigibly plural. I peel and portion
A tangerine and spit the pips and feel
The drunkenness of things being various.

And the fire flames with a bubbling sound for world
Is more spiteful and gay than one supposes—
On the tongue on the eyes on the ears in the palms
    of one's hands—
There is more than glass between the snow and the
    huge roses.

—*Louis MacNeice*

Discouragement is an occupational hazard in my line of work: trying to persuade legislators to enact bigger budgets and stronger standards for children's health. What little progress we achieve seems glacial. (I wonder, will that metaphor be yet another casualty of global warming?)

First taped to my computer and now memorized, this poem helps me keep the faith. Sometimes, when I feel mightily dismayed, I pause to breathe deeply and repeat softly, "May I dwell in possibility." Then I simply do my part and do my best—and trust that good will be the result. When I dwell in possibility, I keep trying, which can be as basic as completing the next task on my list or as challenging as rekindling a sense of possibility among my colleagues.

In communicating about the needs of children, I don't so much try to change someone's mind as to forge connections and find common ground. I try to touch a chord within those with the power to make change.

I've come to see my "occupation" as planting so that others will eventually gather. I plant seeds of ideas and seek to cultivate understanding. I contribute what I can and deeply appreciate the tenacity and passion of those with whom I am privileged to work. Our seeds and strivings will yield results, if not now, then when the time is ripe. It is liberating to work in this way: to relinquish my desire for immediate—or particular—outcomes while remaining open to possibility.

—*Eileen Quinn*

Eileen Quinn is a senior communications officer at PATH, working to reduce global health disparities through ensuring worldwide access to vaccines and other health services. Previously, she was deputy director at the Alliance for Healthy Homes, communications director at the Union of Concerned Scientists, and a producer at C-SPAN.

I dwell in Possibility

I dwell in Possibility –
A fairer House than Prose –
More numerous of Windows –
Superior – for Doors –

Of Chambers as the Cedars –
Impregnable of eye –
And for an everlasting Roof –
The Gambrels of the Sky –

Of Visitors – the fairest –
For Occupation – This –
The spreading wide my narrow Hands
To gather Paradise –

Emily Dickinson

This poem reminds us of the rewards of being fully open to all of life's pain and promise. But the gift of being fully present, "to squeeze inside events," also brings responsibility: to bear witness. Those of us who seek to change the world come to our work with the boldest of ambitions. There will surely be legitimate excuses when we fail. But there are no excuses for not seeing.

In 1984, I was deeply moved by the images of the Ethiopian famine and what I learned about hunger here at home. But what could I do? I realized it wasn't about what I could do alone but what we could do together. With this in mind, I founded Share Our Strength and discovered that there is no limit to the ways in which talented and creative individuals find to share their strength. From chefs cooking at food-and-wine benefits and teaching low-income families nutrition and food-budgeting skills, to medical students spending summers in Ethiopia, assisting in the critical care of those with no other access to health services, there are so many ways to contribute one's own gifts beyond writing a check.

Take the opportunity to contribute in your own way and time. Go somewhere you haven't been and see something you haven't yet seen. Look until you feel something and then tell someone what you've seen and felt and ask them to help bear the load. This is what it takes to change—and be changed by—the world.

—Billy Shore

Billy Shore is the founder and executive director of Share Our Strength, the nation's leading organization working to end childhood hunger in the United States. Shore is also the author of *The Cathedral Within*. In October 2005, *U.S. News & World Report* selected Shore as one of America's Best Leaders.

A Note

Life is the only way
to get covered in leaves,
catch your breath on the sand,
rise on wings;

to be a dog,
or stroke its warm fur;

to tell pain
from everything it's not;

to squeeze inside events,
dawdle in views,
to seek the least of all possible mistakes.

An extraordinary chance
to remember for a moment
a conversation held
with the lamp switched off;

and if only once
to stumble on a stone,
end up drenched in one downpour or another,

mislay your keys in the grass;
and to follow a spark on the wind with your eyes;

and to keep on not knowing
something important.

—Wislawa Szymborska

As a child, one of my favorite picture-books was about Albert Schweitzer in Africa. I loved the pictures of people bringing his pipe-organ, pipe by pipe, into the jungle. Like him, I wanted to make the world a better place but not sacrifice beauty. I chose to do this through working in natural resource management on environmental problems here in the United States.

To my surprise, others saw me as a leader. Having experienced power used to dominate, confuse, and humiliate, I ran in the other direction. But slowly I learned that power with other people is possible and that leadership can be a form of service.

As a university administrator, I used my power to empower others and formed a partnership with a local watershed organization, restoring the commons we shared. And now, as a board member of the Community Food Security Coalition, I am working with allies inside and outside government to increase funds for urban agriculture, farmers' markets, and other ways to support the right to nutritious food for everyone.

When I feel parched and feel I have nothing to give, this song reminds me of the world's beauty surrounding us and gives me the courage to leap back into the struggle for justice with grace. This is when I feel that I have found my work, the reason I am here.

—*Molly D. Anderson*

Molly D. Anderson consults through Food Systems Integrity on science and policy for sustainable food systems and social justice. She was at Tufts University for fourteen years as a faculty member, administrator, community liaison, and researcher. Her professional mission is to promote ecological integrity and justice in food systems.

Replenish

We go on, we go on,
Canoe under hot sun,
The upturned paddle guides liquid to our
    dry mouths.
Water within us, water surrounds us,
A great mystery our becoming dry at all.
Replenish, replenish, all must be
    replenished.
The water within and without.
All that fills us, all that surrounds us:
The great whistling pines,
The tenacious beaver,
The ancient loon,
The rush of the young eagle's wings as it
    dips low over our canoe.
Replenish!
The eyes bathed in this delicate solitude,
This trembling eternity,
Called back in mid-sweep only to be
    assessed by green parched eyes

Replenish!
Each shriveled heart
Which has its moments only at events set
    aside for its song,
But cannot fly for the connection
Between the rock and the human body,
The heron's wing and the hope in our souls.
We go on,
We go on,
Our paddles dance with the lake water to
    the music in our throats.
We will grow dry again
Perhaps leap into the water
A small and symbolic celebration of a great
    and endless task
Which gracefully undertaken,
Might allow us all to go on, and on, and on.

—*Claudia Schmidt*

Carrying the stuff I need to and am good at, and then leaving room for others to carry the stuff that calls to them, is one of the ways I've learned to lead. Nonprofit leadership is about schlepping something somewhere: newsletters, donuts for meetings, giant sticky pads. Shouldering these burdens with ease and humor is a living metaphor for servant leadership, as is the waiting and patience captured in Rosenberg's poem. Robert Greenleaf reminds us, in his great essay on servant leadership, of Milton's rejoinder: "He also serves who stands and waits"—underlining how important it is to offer assistance only when invited rather than inserting oneself with colonial, one-up "help."

I'll never forget the staff meeting where I opined as one of our office norms that "the boss has to be the one who works the longest and the hardest," only to have staff ask why couldn't they ever have a turn at being the star?

The nonprofit sector springs from voluntary association; we need to hold joy as well as effectiveness as a key metric if we want to unleash the potential of people working from their passions. The poem opens with an appreciative breath: "I love how . . ." and then centers itself in celebrating the concrete details of the bags, the burdens shared and collectively carried. Taking the time to both celebrate and name our strengths encourages groups to align from a core of shared spirit, and open to the collective intelligence deeply remembered in the poem's title.

—Ted Lord

Ted Lord is executive director of Humanities Washington. Previously, he served as a partner in Philanthropy Northwest's Giving Practice, where his work as a philanthropic adviser included multiyear change initiatives with Starbucks' and Microsoft's giving programs. In 1999, the Greater Seattle Business Association named him its Community Leader of the Year.

In the End We Are All Light

I love how old men carry purses for their wives,
those stiff light beige or navy wedge-shaped bags
that match the women's pumps,
with small gold clasps that click open and shut.
The men drowse off in medical center waiting rooms,
with bags perched in their laps like big tame birds
too worn to flap away. Within, the wives slowly undress,
put on the thin white robes, consult, come out
and wake the husbands dreaming openmouthed.

And when they both rise up
to take their constitutional,
walk up and down the block, her arms are free as air,
his right hand dangles down.

So I, desiring to shed this skin
for some light silken one,
will tell my husband, "Here, hold this,"
and watch him amble off into the mall among the shining
cans of motor oil, my leather bag
slung over his massive shoulder bone,
so prettily slender-waisted, so forgiving of the ways
we hold each other down, that watching him
I see how men love women, and women men,
and how the burden of the other comes to be
light as a feather blown, more quickly vanishing.

—*Liz Rosenberg*

Standing in the pulpit on Sunday mornings, I often look out and see people who are no longer with us seated in their usual pews. Sitting in the ninth row is John, who died in bed peacefully at ninety early one spring morning. Up in the balcony, Doug is waving to me as I enter, even though he died at fifty-nine of heart failure, leaving behind fourteen-year-old triplets. Absent from her mother's arms is tiny Justine, who died a day before she was due to be born. They are part of all souls and are eternally woven into the story of our community.

Living in and leading a spiritual community comes with the joy and cost of love and mourning. Grace comes through the fluid channels of care, forgiveness, and love that flow below the surface of the healthy congregation, made up of souls, past and present.

I have a vision of the church as a vital instrument of God's love and reconciliation among all people. I engage in a ministry of fierce tenderness by standing with my congregation through life's profound transitions—birth, life, and death.

To work with souls requires access to the ineffable and unnamable; in other words, the sacred in the everyday. Poetry helps us experience these channels. It evokes and embraces that which is universal and unique to our human experience, and I use it in our retreats and wisdom circles. Poetry can help us "remember and forget, forget, remember."

—*Patricia E. de Jong*

Patricia E. de Jong has been the senior minister of the First Congregational Church of Berkeley since 1994. Before coming to Berkeley, she served as minister of education for Christian discipleship at The Riverside Church in New York City. She has been ordained in the United Church of Christ for twenty-seven years.

All Souls

Did someone say that there would be an end,
An end, Oh, an end, to love and mourning?
Such voices speak when sleep and waking blend,
The cold bleak voices of the early morning
When all the birds are dumb in dark November—
Remember and forget, forget, remember.

After the false night, warm true voices, wake!
Voice of the dead that touches the cold living,
Through the pale sunlight once more gravely speak.
Tell me again, while the last leaves are falling:
"Dear child, what has been once so interwoven
Cannot be raveled, nor the gift ungiven."

Now the dead move through all of us still glowing,
Mother and child, lover and lover mated,
And wound and bound together and enflowing.
What has been plaited cannot be unplaited—
Only the strands grow richer with each loss
And memory makes kings and queens of us.

Dark into light, light into darkness, spin.
When all the birds have flown to some real haven,
We who find shelter in the warmth within,
Listen, and feel new-cherished, new-forgiven,
As the lost human voices speak through us and blend
Our complex love, our mourning without end.

—*May Sarton*

I work with many who seek to heal long-standing separation that stalls economic and social progress. This is hard but crucial work. They come from different backgrounds and perspectives; still, they try to move ahead by seeking reconciliation from a collective and painful past.

In one gathering I facilitated a diverse Mississippi group who were working to come to terms with the state's dark history of oppression and injustice. The unhealed tension between two participants—who often faced each other in their world of work—was playing out in our circle. It was evident that they were uncomfortable in each other's presence. Yet during the gathering, they listened to each other. The white male jurist revealed a vulnerable and reflective side no one had seen before and the tough, strong African American woman attorney revealed her heart.

As they struggled with the reality of their history and present day experiences with each other, they listened. A healing unfolded for all of us as we witnessed what was possible in this moment: forgiveness and reconciliation.

On the last day, having listened with compassion and authenticity, they faced each other and talked. They felt safe and risked penetrating barriers that separated them. The power of this experience was indescribable. Tears found their way around the circle. I cried. It was a defining moment.

The retreat concluded. They promised to meet the following week. Wisdom, love, healing, truth, and understanding are possible when we listen deeply.

—*Pat Moore Harbour*

Pat Moore Harbour is the founding director of Healing the Heart of Diversity, a leadership development seminar process that fosters social change leadership and transformative diversity education. She is CEO of the Center for Quality Education.

As a young boy in Amherst, Massachusetts, I lived two blocks from Emily Dickinson's home and walked by it regularly on the way to my best friend's home. But those were the days before Emily was "discovered," though I doubt that discovery would have dazzled this nine-year-old much.

Graduate school filled me with knowledge, but it didn't prepare me for accommodating that learning to the receptivity of my students. It was the blank faces that did that! In learning to respond, I came to understand teaching as more art than science, discerning the needs of individual students, correcting their geometry proofs or essays line-by-line—nudging them toward insight, rather than charismatically holding them spellbound with my dazzle. Just as twilight holds more magic than noonday, so did I come to see that indirection— "telling it slant"—is critical to deepening students' ability to fathom the unfamiliar.

As I have moved from classroom to administration, I have come to see how "telling it slant" is not just a teacher's art but is essential to leaders in any profession. The crux of this art is listening. This means making a concerted effort to hold one's own knowledge and authority in abeyance. Well done, this makes even an ordinary encounter potentially transformative. This is why, decades hence, a student can write and say, "Do you remember that day in the hallway . . . ?"

My admiration for the "gradual dazzlers" of the world is boundless, wherever they are found. They are the great teachers, as well as the great leaders, of the world.

—*Thomas B. Coburn*

Thomas B. Coburn has been president of Naropa University since 2003. Trained as a historian of religion specializing in India, he served on the faculty of St. Lawrence University from 1974 to 2003, where he served as vice president of the university and dean of academic affairs from 1996 to 2002.

Tell all the Truth but tell it slant

Tell all the Truth but tell it slant—
Success in Circuit lies
Too bright for our infirm Delight
The Truth's superb surprise
As Lightning to the Children eased
With explanation kind
The Truth must dazzle gradually
Or every man be blind—

—*Emily Dickinson*

Many of my lessons in leadership have been discovered out on the trail with a team of huskies. I've learned that I can go much further with a team than I can alone. My sled dogs have taught me how leadership can come from unexpected places. A lead dog that is a good trail-breaker may not be the best leader on a hard-packed trail. And those we consider "merely ordinary" team members may just need a chance to flourish. Last spring, one of my "team" dogs took the lead in a blizzard and found the trail home, when my leaders floundered in deep snow. I was stunned to realize that he knew the commands. He was just waiting for the right opportunity to lead.

"The Spell of the Yukon" captures how the North Country can pull you in and not let go. The Arctic has shaped who I am and what I do. The wind-whipping cold, the song of a husky chorus, and the solitude are always calling me home. Living in extreme places has a price; social problems like family violence thrive in isolation. This overwhelming need propelled me into my public health career. From Siberia to the "lower forty-eight" states, I educate communities about the impact of violence on children and integrate lessons from the trail to promote leadership, teamwork, and community collaboration. As a testament to this, a judge in Los Angeles recently wrote that these lessons from the Arctic are helping him make a difference with L.A. city kids.

—Linda Chamberlain

Linda Chamberlain, the founding director of the Alaska Family Violence Prevention Project, is an epidemiologist specializing in childhood exposure to violence and its implications for brain development. A frequent keynote speaker who lives on a homestead outside Homer, Alaska, she holds faculty appointments with the University of Alaska and Johns Hopkins University.

From "The Spell of the Yukon"

The Winter! the brightness that blinds you,
    The white land locked tight as a drum,
The cold fear that follows and finds you,
    The silence that bludgeons you dumb.
    The snows that are older than history,
The woods where the weird shadows slant;
The stillness, the moonlight, the mystery,
    I've bade-em good-bye—but I can't.

There a land where the mountains are nameless,
    And the rivers all run God knows where;
There are lives that are erring and aimless,
    And deaths that just hang by a hair.
There are hardships that nobody reckons;
    There are valleys unpeopled and still;
There's a land—oh, it beckons and beckons,
    And I want to go back—and I will.

—Robert Service

In 1965, following infantry officer, ranger, and paratrooper training, I was assigned to the DMZ in South Korea. After four months as a platoon leader, I was asked to create a human relations program for the ten-thousand-member 2nd Infantry Division—an experience that fundamentally changed my life.

Occupying American soldiers showed little respect for their South Korean hosts, resulting in tension and violence that worked against our shared interest in defending against an invasion by North Korea. Contrary to the advice of superior officers, I initiated a program that brought GI volunteers as English tutors into Korean secondary schools. The program was wildly successful, garnered wide press coverage, and spread throughout South Korea.

The kindness and compassion demonstrated by young soldiers serving as tutors to Korean students touched me deeply. After my experience in Korea, I longed for peaceful options for those who were asking (paraphrasing President John F. Kennedy) what they could do for their country.

Returning to civilian life, I became deeply invested in the work of Martin Luther King Jr. His life and sermon ratified the worthiness of investing a lifetime of service. "Everybody can be great because everybody can serve" has become for me the most emblematic quotation of the service movement in which I have invested my life. It has guided my work in creating opportunities for all youth to find their greatness through service that is lifegiving and who, in turn, are valued as citizens who are needed and respected, no matter their background.

—Jim Kielsmeier

Jim Kielsmeier is founder, president, and CEO of the National Youth Leadership Council (www.nylc.org). He has committed his life to building youth-adult partnerships for community development, civic engagement, and social change that enable young people around the world to grow from being recipients of resources to becoming contributing leaders.

From "The Drum Major Instinct"

If you want to be important—wonderful. If you want to be recognized—wonderful. If you want to be great—wonderful. But recognize that he who is greatest among you shall be your servant. That's your new definition of greatness. And this morning, the thing that I like about it . . . by giving that definition of greatness, it means that everybody can be great. Because everybody can serve. You don't have to have a college degree to serve. You don't have to make your subject and your verb agree to serve. You don't have to know about Plato and Aristotle to serve. You don't have to know Einstein's theory of relativity to serve, you don't have to know the second theory of thermodynamics in physics to serve. You only need a heart full of grace. A soul generated by love. And you can be that servant.

—*Martin Luther King Jr.*

Back At It

William Stafford suggests that a leader resembles a mountain. To be that mountain, you must "accept all that rain and snow," you must "stand there leaning against the wind," you must endure "great stones" tumbling over you that "gouge your sides," and you must be steadfast, even while "a storm" unleashes inside your canyons.

Amidst this churning and grinding, leaders tell us that their most crucial challenge is finding ways to grow and replenish the ineffable sources of their leadership. They describe an approach to leadership not defined by a technique or a process but by a way of being in and with the world animated by the crucial qualities of heart, passion, and connectedness. Their leadership hinges on their capacity to maintain and continuously renew their connections to self and others, even while "leaning against the wind." The core dimensions of leadership are not fixed, indelible qualities impervious to forces that would wear them down. They remain a work in progress that must be tended, restored, and nourished if our leaders are to continuously get back at it—to do the work that must be done.

It is no accident that more leaders identified Tennyson's "Ulysses" than any other poem as the inspiration for their commitments. The poem—and our book—concludes with the line most evoked: "Made weak by time and fate, but strong in will/To strive, to seek, to find, and not to yield."

Thich Nhat Hanh, a Vietnamese Buddhist monk, wrote this poem after American bombers had destroyed a village that he and his monks had helped rebuild four times. He describes tenderly caring for his anger, knowing that it could be turned into action needed for his country's survival.

I became intimate with my own anger in my first year after medical school. The tragic death of a young man, though no one's fault, led to a malpractice suit for me and three other trainees. For weeks, we read awful things about ourselves in the newspaper. I was angry at being unjustly accused. I was angry, too, that there was so little support for us fledgling physicians, and nowhere to go with our feelings or insecurities. No one wanted to talk about it, as if doing so might make them vulnerable as well. Though I was released from the suit, I practiced for years under a cloud of fear. I felt that I couldn't make a mistake, or even look as though I had.

That was over twenty years ago; I no longer feel the weight of fear pervading my decision making, but I know that anger, fear, and loss are rampant in medicine today. Yet physicians adeptly deny these "negative" feelings and fail to deal with them. We need to bring the shadow aspects of our work into the light of day, to attend to them with as much tenderness as we can maintain. We should not be angry at our anger. We can use its energy to transform.

—Henry Emmons, M.D.

Henry Emmons, M.D., is a psychiatric consultant, teacher, and author. He leads retreats for The Inner Life of Healers Renewal Programs through the University of Minnesota's Center for Spirituality and Healing; he wrote *The Chemistry of Joy: A Three Step Program for Overcoming Depression Through Western Science and Eastern Wisdom.*

I grew up in Maine's largest city, but I spent my summers on the old family farm, the last surviving home on a dirt road that one hundred years earlier had twenty-six houses on it. Today, it is my "watering place" for brief retreats from the frenetic activity of my public life, which can often seem to be "too much for us."

Public leaders are more authentic when they do the right thing for the right reasons. This becomes an easier goal when we are rooted in our communities and landscapes, and fully understand our roles and personal motivations.

Just as politics is shaped by our social and natural surroundings, the places we inhabited as children have a lasting emotional hold on us. Over the years my consciousness was woven into the farm, from our first small toy farm animals, to our pick-up baseball games with many cousins, to our annual blueberry-picking gatherings with friends. Today, the familiar landscape brings me peace, and the dramatic busyness of the bird life engages my attention and interest.

In Frost's poem "Directive," personal renewal is not found in wilderness but in a place once inhabited by people living ordinary lives now lost to our understanding. But we know what made their children happy, and our renewal is connected to their experience of living in that place.

Effective public leadership requires personal growth. When we find and go to our own "waters and watering place," we can return for a while to our chosen path "whole again beyond confusion."

—*Tom Allen*

Tom Allen is a six-term congressman, serving the 1st district of Maine. He sits on the Energy and Commerce Committee and concentrates on health care, energy, and environmental issues. To keep his bearings in Congress, he attends weekly "reflection group" gatherings organized by The Faith & Politics Institute.

Directive

Back out of all this now too much for us,
Back in a time made simple by the loss
Of detail, burned, dissolved, and broken off .
Like graveyard marble sculpture in the weather,
There is a house that is no more a house
Upon a farm that is no more a farm
And in a town that is no more a town.
The road there, if you'll let a guide direct you
Who only has at heart your getting lost,
May seem as if it should have been a quarry—
Great monolithic knees the former town
Long since gave up pretense of keeping covered.
And there's a story in a book about it:
Besides the wear of iron wagon wheels
The ledges show lines ruled southeast-northwest,
The chisel work of an enormous Glacier
That braced his feet against the Arctic Pole.
You must not mind a certain coolness from him
Still said to haunt this side of Panther Mountain.
Nor need you mind the serial ordeal
Of being watched from forty cellar holes
As if by eye pairs out of forty firkins.
As for the woods' excitement over you
That sends light rustle rushes to their leaves,
Charge that to upstart inexperience.

Where were they all not twenty years ago?
They think too much of having shaded out
A few old pecker-fretted apple trees.
Make yourself up a cheering song of how
Someone's road home from work this once was,
Who may be just ahead of you on foot
Or creaking with a buggy load of grain.
The height of the adventure is the height
Of country where two village cultures faded
Into each other. Both of them are lost.
And if you're lost enough to find yourself
By now, pull in your ladder road behind you
And put a sign up CLOSED to all but me.
Then make yourself at home. The only field
Now left's no bigger than a harness gall.
First there's the children's house of make-believe,
Some shattered dishes underneath a pine,
The playthings in the playhouse of the children.
Weep for what little things could make them glad.

Then for the house that is no more a house,
But only a belilaced cellar hole,
Now slowly closing like a dent in dough.
This was no playhouse but a house in earnest.
Your destination and your destiny's
A brook that was the water of the house,
Cold as a spring as yet so near its source,
Too lofty and original to rage.
(We know the valley streams that when aroused
Will leave their tatters hung on barb and thorn.)
I have kept hidden in the instep arch
Of an old cedar at the waterside
A broken drinking goblet like the Grail
Under a spell so the wrong ones can't find it,
So can't get saved, as Saint Mark says they mustn't.
(I stole the goblet from the children's playhouse.)
Here are your waters and your watering place.
Drink and be whole again beyond confusion.

—*Robert Frost*

"You have an interstitial lung disease and there isn't anything . . ." I didn't need to hear the rest. My mother had died of the same disease. But I was clear about one thing: I didn't have my mother's resolve to die gracefully and spend my last months preparing my family for life without Mom. I had a strong resolve to live.

The subsequent months brought a successful search for a doctor willing to try new protocols. It was also a time of many questions: "What was the source of my resolve to live?" "Why was I here?" "What does this mean for how I spend the rest of my life?"

My illness was an autoimmune disease triggered by stress, sleep deprivation, and pushing myself too far. And despite all my work to focus on "being" rather than "doing," when faced with death I realized that my being is "doing." How could it be that my need to "do" could also become a source of my death?

Judy Brown's poem helped me through this difficult journey, as I learned to embrace my need to have too many logs burning. As a superintendent of schools, I often found myself responding simultaneously to a child in crisis, a distraught parent, a newspaper reporter at my door, and a spectacular principal on the edge of making a career change because of stress. But what would my life be like if I didn't have that fire that fuels my beliefs and these "doings"? Perhaps that would be a less acceptable form of death.

—Becky van der Bogert

Becky van der Bogert is head of the Palm Beach Day Academy in Palm Beach, Florida. She has served as a public school educator for thirty-eight years and was superintendent in Winnetka, Illinois, for thirteen years. She is committed to creating environments that support educators in pursuit of their passions.

Fire

What makes a fire burn
is space between the logs,
a breathing space.
Too much of a good thing,
too many logs
packed in too tight
can douse the flames
almost as surely
as a pail of water would.

So building fires
requires attention
to the spaces in between,
as much as to the wood.

When we are able to build
open spaces

in the same way
we have learned
to pile on the logs,
then we can come to see how
it is fuel, and absence of the fuel
together, that make fire possible.

We only need to lay a log
lightly from time to time.
A fire
grows
simply because the space is there,
with openings
in which the flame
that knows just how it wants to burn
can find its way.

—*Judy Brown*

In the 1980s, my job as a congressional aide was to help devise a strategy to end the U.S.-backed war in Nicaragua, to stop military aid to the Contras, and to support a peace process in the region.

The wars of those days, like so many wars and so much of politics, were cast in stark polarizing ideologies. Many who held power viewed all such struggles in terms of the Cold War. We fought to define freedom and democracy for others. But how often did we try to understand the lives or the hope stirring in the hearts of those who had long endured repression beyond our imagination?

A friend who was a priest working in the Nicaraguan countryside came to visit me in Washington. He told of Contra attacks in his village and of the funeral mass for the victims. A local woman gave him a message to take up North: "Tell them to send us flowers along with their guns so we can bury our dead."

When he returned to Nicaragua, he left me this poem, written by Nicaraguan poet Daisy Zamora.

As Congress cast vote after vote, sometimes to cut and other times to increase military aid to the contras, I kept this poem at my desk. Through the harsh glare of politics and the embattled night hours, the words of the poet echoed above the cold click of my heels on the marble halls in the U.S. Capitol. Its refrain of "one day . . ." was a song of hope to me.

—Kathleen Gille

Kathleen Gille worked for twenty years for David Bonior, Democratic Whip in the House of Representatives. She has consulted with The Faith & Politics Institute's congressional pilgrimages to Alabama and South Africa, and the Institute for Change of the Service Employees International Union; she is a board member of the Washington Office on Latin America.

Song of Hope

One day the fields will be forever green
the earth black, sweet and wet.
Our children will grow tall upon that earth
and our children's children . . .

And they will be free like mountain trees
and birds.

Each morning they will wake happy to be alive
and know the earth was claimed again for them.

One day . . .

Today we plough dry fields
though every furrow is soaked in blood.

—*Daisy Zamora*

I am an architect, and I teach architecture. I was introduced to Lao Tzu's poem as a young student at the University of Cape Town in South Africa by my teacher. He had been shown the poem by his own teacher, Louis Kahn. Both were great teachers, and both were great architects.

The poem was given to me at a time when I was feeling lost. I was unsure of whether I wanted to continue in architecture. I could not see how its self-centered and self-indulgent design practices could reconcile themselves with the strong call to serve others that I was experiencing.

I was asked to read the poem carefully, to reflect on what I read, and allow the lessons buried in its ancient words to unwrap themselves. They just might, I was told, help me find my way back into architecture again.

The poem revealed that the things I tend to see immediately—the wheel, the pot, the room—are really not the things I need to be paying close attention to. There is always something deeper, more significant, and often magical lurking behind that first appearance, that emerging situation.

Architecture, in its most fundamental sense, became not a physical thing at all but rather a carefully and mindfully wrought spaciousness in which the drama of human life unfolds.

My work and teaching continue to be profoundly marked by this little poem and its call to always help "what's not" become "what is"—that little window into the soul.

—Peter Schneider

Peter Schneider is professor of architecture and Chancellor's Scholar at the University of Colorado. He teaches architectural and environmental history, theory, and design. His scholarly focus is on how the architect's mind, method, and mythologies interact with the natural and cultural landscape and affect the shapes and forms of contemporary architectural practice.

Every Thursday morning when Congress is in session, a small group of members convene in one of our offices to reflect on a reading. We seek ways to respond to the climate—too often mean-spirited and divisive—that pervades Congress. We seek to band together in community for sustenance and courage because the consequences of our decisions are so enormous, the temptations legion. We have discovered the need for grounding is paramount.

One recent morning, Father Clete, from The Faith & Politics Institute, shared the poem "Kindness" with us. Nye's images splintered apart the sequence of our well-ordered resolutions. Her words sent me reeling, dizzy at the edge of a future unknown. I struggled to imagine the possibility for "kindness" in the fractious political debates we have on the floor of the House.

There is a place in me where I have carefully stored my sorrow, protecting it from the layers of sadness I see around me. I avert my gaze. Must I embrace it? Must I know sorrow as the deepest thing before I can find true kindness on the other side? This kindness is, surely, gritty, dripping with sweat, a cup of water offered from one who has known as well great thirst.

After our small group has hugged farewell, I hurry through the airport, eager to return home. I reach into my pocket where the poem is safely tucked. I am ready for the journey. I raise my head, knowing what my eyes are searching for.

—Lois Capps

Lois Capps serves as the representative from California's 23rd congressional district. Before being elected to Congress, Capps was a nurse and health advocate for the Santa Barbara School District for twenty years. She is committed to helping people improve their daily lives through better schools, quality health care, and a cleaner environment.

Kindness

Before you know what kindness really is
you must lose things,
feel the future dissolve in a moment
like salt in a weakened broth.
What you held in your hand,
what you counted and carefully saved,
all this must go so you know
how desolate the landscape can be
between the regions of kindness.
How you ride and ride
thinking the bus will never stop,
the passengers eating maize and chicken
will stare out the window forever.

Before you learn the tender gravity of
    kindness,
you must travel where the Indian in a white
    poncho
lies dead by the side of the road.
You must see how this could be you,
how he too was someone
who journeyed through the night with
    plans
and the simple breath that kept him alive.

Before you know kindness as the deepest
    thing inside,
you must know sorrow as the other deepest
    thing.
You must wake up with sorrow.
You must speak to it till your voice
catches the thread of all sorrows
and you see the size of the cloth.

Then it is only kindness that makes sense
    anymore,
only kindness that ties your shoes
and sends you out into the day to mail
    letters and purchase bread,
only kindness that raises its head
from the crowd of the world to say
It is I you have been looking for,
and then goes with you everywhere
like a shadow or a friend.

—*Naomi Shihab Nye*

While I've taught this poem many times, I always felt this poem was wasted on high schoolers. Sure, it's a great example of device and technique, but I never met a kid who really got the last two lines. Although I could explain them, the kids couldn't feel them. I hope that's less because of my own ineptitude than because the emotion expressed there is one that we only feel as adults, looking back on our naiveté. "What did I know, what did I know?"

As I head into my third decade of adult life, it's not wasted on me. I carry it close to my heart. The speaker's regret reminds me to notice the many acts of love done on my behalf and warns me not to treat them indifferently. It pushes me not merely to be grateful but also to live that gratitude into my relationships. But more than that, this poem really does give me courage.

As a teacher, parent, leader, I always want just the good stuff—the stirring classroom discussion, the laughter over a family board game, the satisfaction that comes when one's vision is realized. My yearning for those golden moments can sometimes blind me to the fact that they don't come without their share of austere and lonely offices. When I do forget, when I find myself chafing at the chores of my life, the speaker's father comes to mind, and his image strengthens me to get about my work. Then I carry on, perhaps without thanks but not without the sense of a love that might one day be appreciated.

—Brian Dunlap

Brian Dunlap taught high school English in four states over a dozen years. He then shifted his professional focus from the students to the people and schools serving them. He has directed certification programs for pre-service and in-service teachers and leads professional and organizational development efforts in Spokane, Washington.

Those Winter Sundays

Sundays too my father got up early
and put his clothes on in the blueblack cold,
then with cracked hands that ached
from labor in the weekday weather made
banked fires blaze. No one ever thanked him.

I'd wake and hear the cold splintering, breaking.
When the rooms were warm, he'd call,
and slowly I would rise and dress,
fearing the chronic angers of that house.

Speaking indifferently to him,
who had driven out the cold
and polished my good shoes as well.
What did I know, what did I know
of love's austere and lonely offices?

—*Robert Hayden*

I often turn to "Tintern Abbey," to find in it the tranquil restoration that the poem itself finds in the scene it contemplates along the river Wye. As a college president embroiled in the noisy life of a college campus, I seek the respite that Wordsworth offers. He shows us how moments of beauty—experienced, remembered, and re-experienced—are woven into the fabric of our being, indeed, help constitute our being. They provide sweet renewal when the weight of the world presses upon us; they inspire a kindly will toward others, and they help us understand the very spirit of the universe.

This poem resonates deeply for me with the world of education I have chosen for my work. We place faith in continuities similar to those Wordsworth describes—between the phases of our experience as human beings, between ourselves and the earth. As educators, we believe that we help shape our students by leading them to moments of contemplation and insight to which they may return, just as I have turned to this poem first as a student, then as a scholar of nineteenth-century poetry, and now as a college president. And we believe in the bond between older and younger with which Wordsworth closes the poem in his address to his sister.

And in moments of "sad perplexity," we return to beauty, as in the landscape Wordsworth describes, or in the poem itself, for the restoration and vision that inspires and blesses us.

—*Carol Tecla Christ*

Carol Tecla Christ is the tenth president of Smith College. She was provost at the University of California, Berkeley. She is a recognized authority on Victorian literature; her books include *Victorian and Modern Poetics*. She is also the editor of *The Norton Anthology of English Literature*.

XXVI
Lines

Composed a Few Miles above Tintern Abbey, on
Revisiting the Banks of the Wye, during a
Tour, July 13, 1798

FIVE years have past; five summers, with the
length
Of five long winters! and again I hear
These waters, rolling from their mountain-
springs
With a soft inland murmur.—Once again
Do I behold these steep and lofty cliffs,
That on a wild, secluded scene impress
Thoughts of more deep seclusion; and
connect
The landscape with the quiet of the sky.
The day is come when I again repose
Here, under this dark sycamore, and view
These plots of cottage-ground, these orchard-
tufts,
Which at this season, with their unripe fruits,
Are clad in one green hue, and lose
themselves
'Mid groves and copses. Once again I see
These hedge-rows, hardly hedge-rows, little
lines
Of sportive wood run wild: these pastoral
farms,
Green to the very door; and wreaths of smoke
Sent up, in silence, from among the trees!
With some uncertain notice, as might seem
Of vagrant dwellers in the houseless woods,
Or of some Hermit's cave, where by his fire
The Hermit sits alone.

These beauteous forms,
Through a long absence, have not been
to me
As is a landscape to a blind man's eye:
But oft, in lonely rooms, and 'mid the din
Of towns and cities, I have owed to them,
In hours of weariness, sensations sweet,
Felt in the blood, and felt along the heart;
And passing even into my purer mind,
With tranquil restoration:—feelings too
Of unremembered pleasure: such, perhaps,
As have no slight or trivial influence
On that best portion of a good man's life,
His little, nameless, unremembered acts
Of kindness and love. Nor less, I trust,
To them I may have owed another gift,
Of aspect more sublime; that blessed mood,
In which the burden of the mystery,
In which the heavy and the weary weight
Of all this unintelligible world,
Is lightened:—that serene and blessed mood,
In which the affections gently lead us on,—
Until, the breath of this corporeal frame
And even the motion of our human blood
Almost suspended, we are laid asleep
In body, and become a living soul:
While with an eye made quiet by the power
Of harmony, and the deep power of joy,
We see into the life of things.
If this
Be but a vain belief, yet, oh! how oft—

In darkness and amid the many shapes
Of joyless daylight; when the fretful stir
Unprofitable, and the fever of the world,
Have hung upon the beatings of my heart—
How oft, in spirit, have I turned to thee,
O sylvan Wye! thou wanderer through the
    woods,
How often has my spirit turned to thee!

And now, with gleams of half-extinguished
    thought,
With many recognitions dim and faint,
And somewhat of a sad perplexity,
The picture of the mind revives again:
While here I stand, not only with the sense
Of present pleasure, but with pleasing
    thoughts
That in this moment there is life and food
For future years. And so I dare to hope,
Though changed, no doubt, from what I was
    when first
I came among these hills; when like a roe
I bounded o'er the mountains, by the sides
Of the deep rivers, and the lonely streams,
Wherever nature led: more like a man
Flying from something that he dreads,
    than one ——
Who sought the thing he loved. For nature
    then
(The coarser pleasures of my boyish days
And their glad animal movements all
    gone by)
To me was all in all.—I cannot paint
What then I was. The sounding cataract

Haunted me like a passion: the tall rock,
The mountain, and the deep and gloomy wood,
Their colors and their forms, were then
    to me
An appetite; a feeling and a love,
That had no need of a remoter charm
By thoughts supplied, nor any interest
Unborrowed from the eye.—That time
    is past,
And all its aching joys are now no more,
And all its dizzy raptures. Not for this
Faint I, nor mourn nor murmur, other gifts
Have followed; for such loss, I would believe,
Abundant recompence. For I have learned
To look on nature, not as in the hour
Of thoughtless youth; but hearing oftentimes
The still, sad music of humanity,
Nor harsh nor grating, though of
    ample power
To chasten and subdue. And I have felt
A presence that disturbs me with the joy
Of elevated thoughts; a sense sublime
Of something far more deeply interfused,
Whose dwelling is the light of setting suns,
And the round ocean, and the living air,
And the blue sky, and in the mind of man:
A motion and a spirit, that impels
All thinking things, all objects of all thought,
And rolls through all things. Therefore am I still
A lover of the meadows and the woods,
And mountains; and of all that we behold
From this green earth; of all the mighty world
Of eye, and ear,—both what they half create,
And what perceive; well pleased to recognise

In nature and the language of the sense,
The anchor of my purest thoughts, the nurse,
The guide, the guardian of my heart,
    and soul
Of all my moral being.
                        Nor perchance,
If I were not thus taught, should I the more
Suffer my genial spirits to decay:
For thou art with me here upon the banks
Of this fair river; thou my dearest Friend,
My dear, dear Friend; and in thy voice
    I catch
The language of my former heart, and read
My former pleasures in the shooting lights
Of thy wild eyes. Oh! yet a little while
May I behold in thee what I was once,
My dear, dear Sister! and this prayer
    I make,
Knowing that Nature never did betray
The heart that loved her; 'tis her privilege,
Through all the years of this our life, to lead
From joy to joy: for she can so inform
The mind that is within us, so impress
With quietness and beauty, and so feed
With lofty thoughts, that neither evil tongues,
Rash judgments, nor the sneers of
    selfish men,
Nor greetings where no kindness is, nor all
The dreary intercourse of daily life,
Shall e'er prevail against us, or disturb
Our cheerful faith, that all which we behold
Is full of blessings. Therefore let the moon
Shine on thee in thy solitary walk;

And let the misty mountain-winds be free
To blow against thee: and, in after years,
When these wild ecstasies shall be matured
Into a sober pleasure; when thy mind
Shall be a mansion for all lovely forms,
Thy memory be as a dwelling-place
For all sweet sounds and harmonies;
    O, then,
If solitude, or fear, or pain, or grief,
Should be thy portion, with what healing
    thoughts
Of tender joy wilt thou remember me,
And these my exhortations! Nor,
    perchance,—
If I should be where I no more can hear
Thy voice, nor catch from thy wild eyes
    these gleams
Of past existence,—wilt thou then forget
That on the banks of this delightful stream
We stood together; and that I, so long
A worshipper of Nature, hither came
Unwearied in that service: rather say
With warmer love,—oh! with far deeper zeal
Of holier love. Nor wilt thou then forget,
That after many wanderings, many years
Of absence, these steep woods and lofty cliffs,
And this green pastoral landscape, were
    to me
More dear, both for themselves and for
    thy sake!

—*William Wordsworth*

American democracy is in trouble. Excessive power is serving the interests of the few to the detriment of the many. As a nation we have strayed so far from our founders' vision of self-governance that the vast majority of citizens no longer believe they can influence our government or make a difference in the direction of our country.

The world is straining from the certainties of leaders who are profoundly out of balance. We all know the difference between power and influence wielded with a hardened heart, compared with power and influence wielded with compassionate open-heartedness. Our times demand that we all bring our whole selves to the task of leadership.

I started AmericaSpeaks to create safe, democratic spaces where all Americans can come together to speak their truth, listen open-mindedly and open-heartedly to others, and together discover their collective voice in service of the common good.

What enables me to risk leadership with compassionate open-heartedness is my deep connection to the natural world. When I despair or am overwhelmed by anger at the injustice running rampant in the world, or lose my perspective on how to make a difference, or lose my faith in humanity, I turn to what has always been the source of greatest nurturance to me. The beauty and wonder of this earth, its mountains, its forests, its waters, its creatures, each and all restore my soul and heal my wounds. "For a time I rest in the grace of the world, and am free."

—Carolyn J. Lukensmeyer

Carolyn J. Lukensmeyer is president and founder of AmericaSpeaks (www.americaspeaks.org), a nonprofit organization working to reinvigorate democracy by engaging citizens in public decision making. She was the first woman chief of staff of the state of Ohio and the deputy project director of Vice President Al Gore's Reinventing Government Task Force.

The Peace of Wild Things

When despair for the world grows in me
and I wake in the night at the least sound
in fear of what my life and my children's lives may be,
I go and lie down where the wood drake
rests in his beauty on the water, and the great heron feeds.
I come into the peace of wild things
who do not tax their lives with forethought
of grief. I come into the presence of still water.
And I feel above me the day-blind stars
waiting with their light. For a time
I rest in the grace of the world, and am free.

—Wendell Berry

Among the wrenching decisions many leaders face is when to step aside to make way for someone else. There's never an easy time to leave work you have loved, people who've become valued partners, even cherished friends, a cause for which you've cared enough to lean patiently against the wind. To let go is to acknowledge that time is running out.

When I decided to step down from a college presidency—a position that had animated and defined me for fourteen years, fueled my energy, my intellect, my passions, opened wide new vistas, reshaped my sense of self—I prefaced my announcement to the trustees by reading them this poem. My words came as a shock, and I'll never forget the sinking feeling that descended on the room as one and then another face registered the news.

They had been telling me they wished I would stay forever, and I had been wanting to believe I could. But there are cycles in organizations, as there are in life, and part of the art of leading well, as of living well, is to recognize new phases struggling to emerge. There comes a time for an organization, and for its leader, to set out on separate paths of self-renewal. And thus began a complex fourteen-month transition, as I led my colleagues toward a bright future in which I would have no place, and myself, alone, into dark canyons to seek out new sources of lightning.

—*Diana Chapman Walsh*

Diana Chapman Walsh was president of Wellesley College from 1993 to 2007. She led major initiatives to enhance campus intellectual life, expand interdisciplinary, experiential, and global learning, and strengthen religious and spiritual life, as well as stewardship of the campus. Formerly, she was a professor and department chair at the Harvard School of Public Health.

Silver Star

To be a mountain you have to climb alone
and accept all that rain and snow. You have to look
far away when evening comes. If a forest
grows, you care; you stand there leaning against
the wind, waiting for someone with faith enough
to ask you to move. Great stones will tumble
against each other and gouge your sides. A storm
will live somewhere in your canyons hoarding its lightning.

If you are lucky, people will give you a dignified
name and bring crowds to admire how sturdy you are,
how long you can hold still for the camera. And some time,
they say, if you last long enough you will hear God;
a voice will roll down from the sky and all your patience
will be rewarded. The whole world will hear it: "Well done."

—William Stafford

In his epic poem, Alfred Lord Tennyson describes the heart, mind, and soul of Ulysses as he decides to venture off on yet another odyssey. After his first voyage, filled with danger, struggle, and accomplishment, Ulysses finds the peaceful life he has earned far too mundane. He summons his aging crew and invites them to join him on one last journey. He assures them that their strong will is enough to carry them through—a message of idealism and hope.

After three decades with a failing heart, rescued by a heart transplant, I felt a shiver of recognition when I first read "Ulysses." My career as the founder and chief executive of Vanguard was over. My first odyssey, filled with cities, men and manners, councils and governments, many honors, and the delight of battle with my peers, had ended. Yet I could not make an end in my own career. With the second chance at life miraculously given to me, I knew that I had to travel as far as my mind and imagination would permit.

So, hoping that "some work of noble note may yet be done," I plunged into a new career. My goals: to build a better mutual fund industry and to return capitalism to its original values, including trusting and being trusted. At the heart of that quest is the idealism that has permeated my life and my conviction that in these remaining years, I must give something back to the world that has given me so much.

—*John C. Bogle*

John C. Bogle founded The Vanguard Group, one of the two largest mutual fund organizations in the world, now managing more than $1 trillion of investor assets. His career has been dedicated to creating a new and better world for mutual fund owners, and for our nation's business and financial systems.

From "Ulysses"

I cannot rest from travel: I will drink
Life to the lees. All times I have enjoy'd
Greatly, have suffer'd greatly, both with those
That loved me, and alone; on shore . . .
I am become a name;
For always roaming with a hungry heart
Much have I seen and known;—cities of men
And manners, climates, councils, governments,
Myself not least, but honor'd of them all,—
And drunk delight of battle with my peers, . . .
I am a part of all that I have met; . . .
How dull it is to pause, to make an end,
To rust unburnish'ed, not to shine in use!
As tho' to breathe were life! Life piled on life
Were all too little, and of one to me
Little remains; but every hour is saved
From that eternal silence, something more,
A bringer of new things; . . .
And this gray spirit yearning in desire
To follow knowledge like a sinking star,
Beyond the utmost bound of human thought. . . .
      There lies the port; the vessel puffs her sail;
There gloom the dark, broad seas. My mariners,
Souls that have toil'd, and wrought, and thought with me,—
That ever with a frolic welcome took
The thunder and the sunshine, and opposed
Free hearts, free foreheads,—you and I are old;
Old age hath yet his honor and his toil.

Death closes all; but something ere the end,
Some work of noble note, may yet be done, . . .
        Come, my friends,
'Tis not too late to seek a newer world.
Push off, and sitting well in order smite
The sounding furrows; for my purpose holds
To sail beyond the sunset . . . until I die. . . .
Tho' much is taken, much abides; and tho'
We are not now that strength which in old days
Moved earth and heaven, that which we are,
we are,—
One equal temper of heroic hearts,
Made weak by time and fate, but strong in will
To strive, to seek, to find, and not to yield.

—Alfred Lord Tennyson

Leading with Fire

USING POETRY IN OUR LIFE AND WORK

A poet is a person who "lets drop a line that gets remembered in the morning."
—*E. B. White[1]*

ike most leaders, the men and women in this book put a premium on action. They are healers, politicians, activists, educators, organizers, and entrepreneurs. Though disparate in profession, their stories—one and all—describe a quest to act from principles and to be leaders whose actions are intentional, conscious, and authentic. Carrying out these aspirations amidst the frenetic demands of the workplace, the bottom-line pressures of institutions, and the disorienting and blurred boundaries between home and work is awesomely difficult. If leaders are to do their best and most inspired work in service of others and to the causes that drive their effort, they must continually engage in the crucial task of attending to who they are and how they want to be with others.

Poetry, the leaders told us, helps them to make these important connections. It enables them to excavate their beliefs, stay grounded, and renew their heart. Poetry read with intention serves as a prism for self-study. They read it in private for pleasure or solace, and with their colleagues to invite creative thinking and evoke conversations that matter.

A review of the vast literature on leadership reveals hundreds of theories and approaches to the craft, science, and art of leadership. It is a much-explored area that has given rise to countless leadership development programs, classes, seminars, and books designed to help individuals develop the skills and capacities necessary to guide themselves and influence others. Synthesizing this wide range of writings on leadership, we have identified six central tasks that all leaders face. This chapter explores how poetry can be used to support a leader's effort in each of these crucial endeavors:

1. Leaders Find and Listen to Their Inner Voice
2. Leaders Listen and Attend to Others
3. Leaders Tell Stories and Inspire Shared Vision
4. Leaders Cultivate an Organization's Creative Imagination
5. Leaders Evoke Conversations That Matter
6. Leaders Foster Renewal

Leaders Find and Listen to Their Inner Voice

Leadership is so busy, so public, so open to scrutiny that there is often little space or opportunity for the intimate, pensive conversations with self. The leaders in this book described the special role that poetry plays in providing those private, personal encounters with self. They described a multitude of heartbreaking and sustaining conversations between themselves and the poems in their life. It was clear that these conversations were both deep and unfathomably important.

Finding Poems That Matter

The respondents in the book have found their way past the trauma of high school English and the dreaded formal explication and exegesis of poetry. They described themselves as poetry collectors and poetry traders. Some have voluminous computer files of poetry; others copy favorite poems down into elegant leather-bound journals; others memorize poems, and still others carry them in wallets or electronic organizers.

These leaders are passionate about poetry because it awakens something inside them. The language they used to detail their encounters with their cherished poems was poetic itself. They didn't describe their "systematic process of analysis" or their "approach to dismembering and deconstructing the text" but told how they fell in love with a poem, or how a jarring collision with a poem stood them up straight, or how a poem entangled their soul, yielding insights into self and their work. They described their relationship to poetry as playful, challenging, and intimate. Several suggested that their orientation to poetry could best be understood through a poem written by Billy Collins—one of our recent poet laureates—fittingly called "Introduction to Poetry."[2]

Introduction to Poetry

I ask them to take a poem
and hold it up to the light
like a color slide

or press an ear against its hive.

I say drop a mouse into a poem
and watch him probe his way out,

or walk inside the poem's room
and feel the walls for a light switch.

I want then to water-ski
across the surface of a poem
waving at the author's name on the
    shore.

But all they want to do
is tie the poem to a chair with a rope
and torture a confession out of it.

They begin beating it with a hose
to find out what it really means.

                —Billy Collins

Using Poems as Companions

For these leaders, their poems were not just dalliances but long-time companions on their leadership journey. Bernard Josefsburg described how he first read Richard Wilbur's "The Beautiful Changes" as a young high school English teacher with his students, then as a young groom at his wedding; then he came back to it as a "much older school superintendent, charged with saying wise things to students at their high school graduation."

Others, like Rachel Boechler, described how the unique and mysterious quality of poetry can serve one's vocational journey. "I cannot identify one poem or means of using poetry that guides me . . . this changes as I change and grow as a leader. I only know that poetry is my faithful companion in staying true to what is true for me—and ideally what is true for others as they too search for the deeper meaning of their work in this world."

Waking Yourself Up with a Poem

The right poem encountered at the right time is a gift. Keats described the experience of reading certain poems as evoking a feeling akin to a "spear going through me." John Dewey described the reading of poetry as causing physical symptoms such as "bristling of the skin, shivers in the spine, constrictions of the throat and a feeling in the pit of the stomach."[3]

Many of our contributors reach for poetry as a bracing and welcome interruption to the harriedness of life. Our leaders described using poetry to attend to what was happening inside themselves.

Pastor Bill White, who serves a busy urban church in Los Angeles, has adopted the practice of waking up each morning and reciting poetry to orient his day. He has memorized a dozen or so poems that set his day in motion, pointing him down the path of peace. "Walking down the hallway, with my family sound asleep, I recite an ancient psalm like, 'Out of the depths I cry to you O Lord. O Lord hear my prayer.' The words form a melody that helps me clear away the night's fog and awaken with hope, focus, and resolve."

Others keep poetry anthologies on their night stand or around their desk so they can forage for a poem when they need it. Ted Lord wrote, "I have a book of poetry collected by Garrison Keillor on my desk at home. I am apt to pick it up when I need a break, when I experience an impasse, when I am beginning to prepare a program or a talk. Sometimes a line or a couplet supports my own process and turns my thinking in wondrous ways."

Small-business owner Linda Wolfe begins each morning in meditation with a poem before she heads to work. "I have a small journal in which I write special poems or prayers and usually choose one or two to read as a focal point for my meditation. I like that this little beautiful book contains only pieces that really speak to me and that they are in my own handwriting."

Other leaders subscribe to listservs that provide a "poem a day" to their e-mail box; here are a few of their favorites:

- Robert Pinsky's Favorite Poem Project includes videos of poems being read (http://www.favoritepoem.org/thevideos/index.html).

- There are poetry readings from Bill Moyers's Fooling with Words (http://www.pbs.org/wnet/foolingwithwords/).
- The Academy of American Poets has a listening booth where you can hear poets read their work (http://www.poets.org/).
- Garrison Keillor reads a poem a day at the Writer's Almanac (Garrison Keillor's "The Writer's Almanac," http://www.writersalmanac.org/).

Using Poems as Talismans

A talisman is a small, cherished object intended to bring good luck and protection to its owner. Leaders shared how certain poems occupy this role in their life—poems to ward off the incursions of fear, loneliness, and isolation. Sara Sanders, the chair of the English, Communication and Journalism Department at Coastal Carolina University, describes how she keeps a copy of Rumi's "This Being Human Is a Guest House" under her desk blotter: "I read it every morning when I come into the office and before or after challenging events to remind me that there is a gift in everything that comes during the day."

Talismans can also help to ground us or give us reason to pause. Eileen Quinn writes, "I keep a poem on the wall near my desk. It helps me to remember, when I lift my eyes from the work (frenzy) of the moment, that there is a wide world out there, and much more to life than the challenge at hand. On occasion, I change poems, so that I have a new perspective after a while."

Leaders Listen and Attend to Others

People yearn to be heard. From teenagers, to middle-level managers, to the infirm in hospital beds, to politicians on the floor of the statehouse, there is a yearning to be taken seriously, to be respected, to be attended to by another. Many of the professionals from physicians to CEOs described how they need to continually discipline themselves to listen. As one leader said, "The best ideas do not come from leaders but from customers and people working on the factory floor or in the salesroom." Others told us of how they worked with their leadership and management teams to develop a collective habit of deep listening.

Leaders described how their practice with poetry exercises their "listening muscles." They described practicing habits that opened them up to be more receptive and less judgmental. As Paul Batalden, a physician, told us, "A poem gives me permission to invite careful consideration of something. It allows me to invite the careful, creative attention of people. So, when I use a poem in a class or in an orientation session or a speech or a meeting, I am aware that I am inviting generative, creative people to join me. Using the poem often has a two-fold effect: one on the listener and one on me. The effect on me is to be even more careful of the invitation I am extending to others. The space poems help create remind me of the respect I need to be fully present."

Several leaders described how poetry serves as an antidote to the default mode of listening in organizations, which tends to be intensely critical and judgmental—listening so that you can hear the problem, discern the issue, and then proffer solutions that will resolve the problem. It's about listening to fix, advise, and solve. Caryl Hurtig Casbon describes a process that invites leaders from across professions to consider an alternative mode of paying attention. "So many leaders believe that giving advice and fixing problems is their job. However, we all know how often the advice and the best counsel offered don't lead to solutions." Casbon describes an alternative process of teaching leaders to ask open and honest questions: "I work with leaders using the poem 'When Someone Deeply Listens to You.' The poem resonates with leaders, for in our fast-paced world, we realize how rare it is to slow down and truly listen to one another. It names a hunger we all share—to be heard."

When Someone Deeply Listens to You

When someone deeply listens to you
it is like holding out a dented cup
you've had since childhood
and watching it fill up with
cold, fresh water.
When it balances on top of the brim,
you are understood.
When it overflows and touches your skin,
you are loved.

When someone deeply listens to you
the room where you stay
starts a new life
and the place where you wrote
your first poem
begins to glow in your mind's eye.
It is as if gold has been discovered!

When someone deeply listens to you
your bare feet are on the earth
and a beloved land that seemed distant
is now at home within you.

—John Fox

Casbon follows reading the poem with inviting participants to ask each other honest and open questions—ones that respect the integrity of the other person by not imposing judgments, opinion, or advice.

Many health care professionals described how their encounters with poetry help them not only attend more deeply to their patients but attend to the often confusing emotions and suppressed feelings of grief, sadness, and guilt that they experience when working with the sick and dying.

A compelling example of this practice is under way at Columbia University Medical Center, where physician Bert Bregman has instituted the reading and writing of poetry into the routine of the interns he supervises during their internal-medicine rotation. The approach is

> part of a new trend in medical education known as "narrative medicine"—listening to and then writing down patients' stories, as opposed to jotting a shorthand list of their symptoms. . . . This encourages the students to see patients as people, not "the gall bladder in Room 31," and can tease out nuances of symptoms, habits, and feelings that can help doctors determine appropriate treatment. . . . The students see intense family and patient inter-actions. They are stuffed with impressions that they don't have a place to express. Reading and writing poetry can create that place. We teach them to pay attention to the way the poem looks on the page, to be aware of rhyme and line endings. I want the poems to make us slow down and listen.[4]

Selecting the Right Poem

Many of those who work with poetry describe how critical it is to find the right poem. Rick Jackson, codirector of the Center for Courage & Renewal, recommends the following steps for selecting the right poem and choosing questions that invite deep listening to the poem.

- Is it relatively brief and to the point? Sometimes longer poems can work if there is enough relevant content; in general, however, overly lengthy and wordy poems can cause people to get bogged down or lose interest.

- Is it accessible? Look for imagery that allows one to easily enter into the poem and for language that is easy to understand.

- Does the poem contain aspects of both the personal and the universal? Will it allow for the exploration of the "little" stories of individuals while also being capable of expanding to encompass larger archetypal themes?

- Is there enough in the way of mystery, of rich content, or connection to inner dilemmas? Some poems are so straightforward and obvious that they don't readily lend themselves to lengthier exploration.

- When selecting poems or stories, make sure to choose materials that come from diverse voices, cultures, and perspectives.

Asking Questions That Invite Engagement with the Poem

Here are some effective questions for cultivating fruitful interactions between the readers and the text:

- What do you notice in this poem?
- Where does this poem intersect with your life?
- What initially attracted you to this poem?
- What is happening in this poem and to whom?
- What do you find elusive or opaque?
- What do you sense this poem is trying to tell you?
- What images, words, or phrases seem to linger in your mind?
- Who would you give this poem to and why?

Processing the Experience

There are many ways to do this. Sometimes you can have everyone sit in silence; sometimes you can ask participants to "freewrite." In a freewriting exercise, participants sit down with the poem and simply write without stopping for a set amount of time. This is a nonthreatening, freewheeling way to generate lots of ideas and disarm some of the anxiety that people may have about discussing poetry. Through freewriting, ideas emerge and threads of meaning can be uncovered. After a freewrite, it can be effective to meet in small groups of two or three to speak about what was raised for the writers before returning to the larger group.

By way of a more concrete example, here is a poem and a series of questions that Jackson often uses to invite the careful listening to self: "We begin with reading 'The Way It Is' then, we will sit in silence for a brief time to reflect on its meaning in our lives and consider the following questions: What are some threads—personal beliefs and convictions—that you try to hold on to in your life and work? What helps you to hold on to them? What makes it difficult to hold on? What inner resources serve to sustain you?"

Leaders Tell Stories and Inspire Shared Vision

To be effective, every leader must tell stories and understand how to wield expressive language and vivid imagery. Leaders must tell stories of who they are and the values they hold. They must tell stories of where the organization is at that moment in time, and they must build a shared vision for where they are headed.

Dozens of leaders wrote that they use poetry to enhance their ability to share who they are with those they work with and serve. Tom Vander Ark, president of X Prize Foundation, described poetry as indispensable in helping him "get deep fast" in his talks and other public presentations. "Most staff meetings are superficial and administrative. To get to the heart of the matter and do so within the constraints of schedules . . . leaders need strategies for going deep fast. Some people are skilled facilitators; some use books, some stories, some videos. For me, poetry is the most authentic (and effective) way to reach unexpressed memory—fear, doubt, anger, delight, awe, wonder—and make conversational the unmentionables."

Linda Chamberlain, an Alaskan epidemiologist who speaks to audiences across the world about the ravages of domestic violence, discovered that a way to grip her audience from the outset is to use poetry: "A few years ago, a survivor of severe domestic violence gave me a poem written by her daughter, who also grew up in terror as a victim of incest. The daughter had become severely obese as a child; she developed hypertension and was sent to the top specialists, but to no avail. It wasn't until she started journaling and writing poetry (after going 'underground' with her mother to escape the violence) that she was able to disclose the sexual abuse and the anger, and start the journey of healing. I use her poem frequently (and anonymously). It's called 'There's Goes the Light in the Hallway' and describes in no way that I ever could the terror of what happened in that home after the lights went out."

Sterling Speirn, president of the Kellogg Foundation, uses poetry to open important conversations in various settings: "I like Wislawa Szymborska's 'A Word on Statistics' for almost any occasion, and I use Dana Gioia's 'Money,' often when I start out a speech talking about Dwight McDonald's comment many decades ago that private foundations are nothing but a big pile of money completely surrounded by people who want some. And Naomi Shihab Nye's 'Kindness' is also one I like to share whenever I want to balance the natural do-goodedness of foundation efforts with an acknowledgment of sadness and loss and suffering."

Howie Shaffer, director of public outreach for the Public Educational Network (PEN), wrote: "I frequently use poetry to promote an emotional understanding of the intellectual concepts that I am trying to convey. In school reform, too often we appeal to the head and not to the heart. At PEN, we use poetry in almost all of our communications; we have used poetry in annual reports, board meeting minutes, weekly e-newsletters, congressional testimony, commencement speeches and research reports. Poetry importantly reminds us that we share common hopes, dreams, fears, and joys. Typically, after giving a speech, people will comment on the beautiful selection of poetry. In this regard, what is most memorable for many listeners is not technical information but the reminder of the beauty of togetherness, our oneness, and our fundamental interrelatedness."

For leaders seeking language and images that conjure up emotion and insight to inspire others, poetry can be a powerful tool. Poetry traffics in memorable metaphors and uses language that emboldens our imaginative capacities and invites us to envision complexities and subtleties. If we think of great speeches we have heard over the years, what stays with us are those word images that excite our imagination. Peter Karoff, founder and chairman of The Philanthropic Initiative, told us, "I will often meet people who say, 'I heard you speak at the X meeting a few years ago—are you still doing the poetry thing?' In other words, they can't remember any of my 'brilliant' comments, but they do remember there was poetry in the room. More evidence of how much we need just that in our lives."

Lee Rush described how he uses a poem like Billy Collins's "On Turning Ten" to provide a story-metaphor for a workshop on school programs: "The poem gets people into their hearts right away, much better than throwing up a PowerPoint slide to start. Reading poetry at the beginning of a talk is like tilling and plowing a field . . . making it possible to open hearts, so one can plant seeds of hope and wisdom, making it possible for a future harvest of new ideas and actions to occur. Then as people leave and go 'back out into the world,' reading a poem is like applying a dressing on a wound . . . to hold the heart open enough to heal and to protect it, enough medicine for the soul to keep away germs of cynicism."

Jim Kielsmeier illustrated how poetry can be used in the stories leaders tell: "I have learned to use poetry as a kind of punctuation for a story told publicly, say, in a formal presentation. It can bring listeners to pause and gather in, or perhaps become suddenly more alert as if an exclamation point."

Leaders Cultivate an Organization's Creative Imagination

Creativity and innovation is at the heart of leadership. Across professions our leaders told us that poetry was a powerful catalyst for inspiring daring and innovative thinking within the organization.

Several leaders described poetry as vital in getting themselves and others to move beyond rational, strategic, and methodical ways of thinking. Irene Martin shared that "In addition to reading poetry, I write poetry about issues I struggle with, to try to engage them in a different part of my brain and see what new insight emerges. Searching for the exact word and image to convey thoughts and feelings with economy can help clarify complex issues and reduce them to their essential core."

Karen Lee Turner transitions a group to more creative thinking through an activity that invites them to take in disparate information and then organize it creatively and poetically. "When I'm leading a group (class, retreat, organizational meeting, and so on) I like to get others involved in poetry by asking them to read a current newspaper article (or in some cases their own mission statement) and then write a poem in response to what they've read."

Cindy Johnson, who works with a range of organizational leaders, described a process for evaluating progress on goals and objectives using a poetic parable to encourage the interaction of creative stories among those in an organization. Her objective is to use the power of story and poetic language to stimulate the individual and collective imagination of the organization. The poetic parable reads:

> The story is told of a South American tribe that went on a long march, day after day, when all of a sudden they would stop walking, sit down to rest for a while, and then make camp for a couple of days before going any farther. They explained that they needed the time of rest so that their souls could catch up with them.

Johnson then had the group talk about what happens when you sit around the campfire with fellow travelers. They talked of storytelling and began to share stories associated with their work together. They also talked about the wisdom that comes from such stories—wisdom that can (and did) inform next steps on their journey into the future of their organization.

Leaders Evoke Conversations That Matter

Many of the leaders described using poetry to deepen the discourse, inspire imaginative thought, and build connections. While most meetings focus on tasks, strategy, and planning, poetry can evoke the often-hidden dormant imagination of individuals and organizations alike. As Henri Nouwen reminds us, "We cannot change the world by a new plan, project, or idea. We cannot even change other people by our convictions, stories, advice, and proposals, but we can offer space where people are encouraged to disarm themselves, lay aside their occupations and preoccupations and listen with attention and care to the voices speaking in their own center."[5]

One particularly powerful example was described by Winnetka, Illinois, superintendent Becky van der Bogert, who searched for a way to open a conversation about a raw and painful wound in her district. For a year following a near teachers' strike, Becky was holding full responsibility for what she saw as a failure. After meeting with several consultants, she became convinced that the district wouldn't heal until she shared how painful the process had been for her and that everyone needed to work together to heal.

In her opening day address to over three hundred staff members, she shared the poem "It Is I Who Must Begin" by Vaclav Havel. After emphasizing the lines, "I am neither the only one nor the first, nor the most important to set out upon this road," the poem enabled everyone to listen intently and nondefensively, as she shared her journey through the pain. She followed with her realization that it was an arrogance on her part to think that she was totally responsible for what happened, and an invitation to everyone to join in to share the healing process. After a standing ovation, everyone recognized that it was time to begin talking about the near-strike.

Sometimes, poems challenge leaders to bring more of themselves to their work. Terell P. Lasane wrote: "As a college educator and a student affairs professional, I have engaged in a great deal of reflection about how much I should disclose about myself and whether my multiple minority identities should inform the way I approach my work. Lucille Clifton's poem clarifies any ambiguity about the great power that I have and should use: it is both my gift and responsibility to describe my triumphs over the adversity rendered by the unique layers of my personal identity as a minority leader in higher education."

"won't you celebrate with me. . . ."

won't you celebrate with me
what i have shaped into
a kind of life? i had no model.
born in babylon
both nonwhite and woman
what did i see to be except myself?

i made it up
here on this bridge between
starshine and clay,
my one hand holding tight
my other hand; come celebrate
with me that everyday
something has tried to kill me
and has failed.

—Lucille Clifton

Using Poetry to Interrupt the Routine.

Chaos and intensity can become routine for leaders. Crisis and urgency becomes the norm. Over time people can become depleted, disenchanted, and detached from themselves and each other. Poetry can be used to interrupt the frenetic pace and invoke a change of tempo, a moment of stillness amidst the hurly-burly.

Several submitters described how they use poetry to interrupt a group's routine. One administrator described how in long, painful meetings, he sometimes interrupts the grind of deliberations to read a poem. "In the middle of those painful budget discussions, I'll sometimes just whip out a poem. At first, they thought I was crazy, but it changes the logic and infuses some humanity back into the work."

Jim Autry, a former Fortune 500 executive who now writes about leadership and works with leaders, says, "I have used poetry in my conversations, presentations, and workshops for many years. In fact, these days, I begin every presentation with a poem. It changes the atmosphere; it moves people from their constantly racing 'monkey brain' to a deeper place. It makes them more receptive to what comes next because they are not only thinking about the material but also feeling its impact on them."

Autry also describes this: "When doing a workshop or retreat, I do a technique called the poetry bazaar. (I borrowed this idea from someone else.) I have printed sections or lines from poems from many sources: classical, mystical, formal, narrative, and so on. I lay these out on several tables; then give the meeting attendees twenty or thirty minutes to meander from table to table, reading the poetry. They are to find one that speaks deeply to them and take it back to their seats. When ready, I ask people to volunteer to read what they've selected and tell the group why it speaks to them. I've done this with all kinds of groups, from corporate leaders to educators to church leaders to elected officials. You would be absolutely amazed at the emotional impact this little exercise has. It moves the group to a different place in relating to one another."

Barbara Hummel has discovered that poetry can help catalyze a breakthrough at an impasse: "I'm often brought in when groups feel stuck, want to make faster progress, or have some issue that feels difficult to discuss. In calling them to work that is difficult or feels risky, I want to set a tone that helps them name what is true for them and not feel they'll be punished or shamed. I harbor no illusions that this is easy work for them; truth tellers can have limited longevity in some organizations, and yet if the truth goes underground, progress can't fully blossom. I go slowly at first, setting up ground rules so that people know how we will proceed. Slowly these meetings start to take on an aliveness: people, in small ways, begin to speak their truth. I work hard to hear and acknowledge what they are saying, especially if it's difficult news, as these comments help identify some of the sticking points to progress. The poems I most often use at the end of a meeting of difficult conversations are 'Full and Empty' (Laurie Shiparski) or 'Patient Trust' (Pierre Teilhard de Chardin). I usually say a few words first, acknowledging the hard work they've done. Then, I give each person a copy of the poem, and read it, leaving a short period of silence. The other poem.

I have frequently used to open a time that is a continuation of difficult work is Wendell Berry's 'Purification.' After reading that, I invite people to write down what they need to put in their trench so the meeting can be constructive."

Leaders Foster Renewal

Leaders must find respite in the whirlwind. They need to develop habits that restore energy and vitality amidst the buffeting forces of busyness and intensity that mark the ambiguous, result-driven, and highly pressurized contexts of their work. Our contributors struggle with sustaining the gifts and practices that are the core of their work. They described feeling stretched and depleted and searching for ways to stay fresh and alive in their work.

A poignant example of how poetry can support leaders seeking renewal, comes from The Faith & Politics Institute where members of Congress meet in weekly reflection groups designed to provide occasions for quiet reflection, spiritual community, and contemplative dialogue. These group meetings allow individuals to reflect alongside one another, learn from each other, support one another, and engage in meaningful conversation about values and beliefs in connection with their roles in Washington.

As Doug Tanner explained, poetry plays a big part in'these gatherings: "In early morning meetings of small 'reflection groups' I have used poetry to help members of Congress and other harassed, harried, preoccupied people on Capitol Hill find a still point from which to take stock of their days and decisions. We begin weekly one-hour meetings with a few minutes of silence, broken by a poem or a brief prose reading. The conversation that follows goes where the spirit leads, usually to places of considerable depth."

Marcy Jackson, codirector, Center for Courage & Renewal, uses Stanley Kunitz's poem "The Layers" to help leaders intentionally renew their spirit and reconnect who they are with what they do. The process begins with a reading and concludes with some guiding questions.

The Layers

I have walked through many lives,
some of them my own,
and I am not who I was,
though some principle of being
abides, from which I struggle
not to stray.
When I look behind,
as I am compelled to look
before I can gather strength
to proceed on my journey,
I see the milestones dwindling
toward the horizon
and the slow fires trailing
from the abandoned camp-sites,
over which scavenger angels
wheel on heavy wings.
Oh, I have made myself a tribe
out of my true affections,
and my tribe is scattered!
How shall the heart be reconciled
to its feast of losses?
In a rising wind
the manic dust of my friends,
those who fell along the way,
bitterly stings my face.
Yet I turn, I turn,
exulting somewhat,
with my will intact to go

wherever I need to go,
and every stone on the road
precious to me.
In my darkest night,
when the moon was covered
and I roamed through wreckage,
a nimbus-clouded voice
directed me:
"Live in the layers,
not on the litter."
Though I lack the art
to decipher it,
no doubt the next chapter
in my book of transformations
is already written.
I am not done with my changes.[6]

—Stanley Kunitz

After reading the poem out loud, Jackson invites them to reflect on the poem in silence or through open-response journal writing and then leads a discussion using the guiding questions below. The questions are open-ended but ask the leaders to consider what it means to lose and find one's vocational passion across the stretch of time and to consider how one's commitment and relationship to vocation is not a fixed, indelible condition but a state that ebbs and flows with the context and challenges of a leader's life.

- What stands out for you in this poem? Some words or phrases?
- What in this poem speaks to your own experience?

- How does looking back strengthen us to move forward again?
- What might it mean to "live in the layers and not on the litter?"

At a time when social and organizational problems are most often treated as technocratic puzzles to be solved by external solutions or by short-term tinkering with the system, the leaders in this volume describe their desire to create organizations that are rigorous, relational, and devoted to doing worthy work.

They know that in our ultra-busy, competitive, and desperately breathless world, we need tools that slow us down, talk to our heart, and inspire conversations, both within ourselves and with others, about what it means to lead, to serve, and to journey with heart. They understand that we do our best work when we are inspired, challenged, and absorbed in the perplexing but essential conversations about the meaning of our lives and work.

In hearing the many stories of leaders striving to serve well, it is clear that to do their best work, leaders must devise ways to keep their own heart alive and discover ways to forge common cause through public words, shared images, and collective action. These thoughtful leaders reach for poetry as an alternative to the mechanical and the over-rational. They seek poetry for the wild and potent magic it brings into the work of leadership. They turn to poetry for its power to evoke what is best in ourselves and in others.

Notes

1. Cited in Grisham, T. (2006). Metaphor, poetry, storytelling and cross-cultural leadership. *Management Decision, 44*(4), 486–503.

2. Collins, B. *The apple that astonished Paris: Poems.* Fayetteville: University of Arkansas Press, 1988, p. 58.

3. Dewey, J. (1958). *Art as experience.* New York: Putnam, p. 216. (Original work published 1934)

4. Grace, O. C. (2004, November-December). Medicine and metaphor [electronic version]. Duke Magazine, *90*(6). Retrieved March 1, 2007.

5. Nouwen, H.J.M. (1975). *Reaching out: The three movements of the spiritual life.* Garden City, NY: Doubleday, p. 76.

6. *The Collected Poems of Stanley Kunitz.* New York: W. W. Norton, 2000.

Afterword
by David Whyte

$\mathcal{G}$ive me a place to stand and I will move the world," announced Archimedes, over two thousand years ago, proud of his newly minted and newly poetic understanding of the lever and the fulcrum. He himself stood at the dawn of our empirical understanding of the world—a world we as a species wanted to lever in directions that were more predictable, more ordered—more beneficial to human want.

Two thousand four hundred years after that line was uttered, Archimedes might be more than a little frightened at just how easily human beings can now move their world, how many points of leverage we have gained over our surroundings, and how often we use those levers for a small advantage while losing sight of a larger, immovable world that is necessary to our happiness. Like an empire initially sure of itself, then breasting the wave of history through its own momentum, and, finally, losing a sense of forward motion, we have now become rightly unsure of ourselves as purely strategic, empirical beings, destined to carve out a successful place for ourselves in an increasingly complex world.

Firstly and disturbingly, we are just beginning to understand that many of our strategic and empirical gifts and many of our historically accepted virtues around hard work are actually making the world a more hostile place, emotionally, environmentally, and socially. Secondly, work itself and our sense of participation in work can no longer be blithely accepted as a good in itself. We only have to take a single step back from the perspective of personal ambition to see that much of our accepted understanding of good work is actually tearing at the biological fabric of life as we know it. What we have come to think of as good leadership, therefore, merely tied to our old, unthinking goals without this larger context, may simply be leading us off the cliff edge of human history all the faster.

I recount the difficulties of our present time, not as an excuse for wailing and passivity but as a way of finding a different kind of leverage, to gain, in effect, another place to stand and as a way to reflect on *Leading from Within*. This book carries the poet's perspective that the language we have inherited in our present time, especially in our present workplace, gives us far too little leverage over the central dynamics that are a key to human happiness and satisfaction. It takes the stance that the present, seemingly mighty flow of information is actually too small a stream to represent that other wide river of imaginative inheritance that flows behind us and that might float us into the future we want for ourselves.

The poetry in *Leading from Within* is constantly attempting to lead us back to this inheritance, this grand perspective, this wide horizon—to the ecological view of human beings that says we are made up of many streams, many of them invisible and rarely articulated, and that by our overspecialization in making, getting, and spending, we construct a life of exile that simply creates more and more thirst, demanding more and more surface irrigation to cover up the increasing suspicion that we are actually drinking less and less from the tributaries that matter.

William Stafford's "Listening" invites us to experience silence not as a lack of sound but as an invitation to worlds that are overwhelmed by our constant need to speak. Mary Oliver's "Spring Azures" conjures the image of Blake as a child, seeing God fluttering up through the dirt and grime of industrial London. Shakespeare's famous "Sonnet 29" re-imagines memory, not as factual recall but as a return to sanity. It looks at the temptation of those, even of the greatest talent, to compare themselves with others and the way happiness returns through the ability to return to the integrative, abiding themes of human life.

There is another focused, practical dynamic evident in the poetry that speaks to those who are students of leadership: the underlying foundation that sustains the palpable sense of belief that most good leaders exhibit. This foundation is not usually a facile set of inherited notions to which a leader must stick through thick and thin but an identity formed through refusing the easy answer. It is a way of holding seemingly discordant elements together by making the conversation between seeming contradictions everyday and real. A good leader holds together private ambition and public good, personal happiness and service to others, long-term profit with short-term losses, the difficult promises made to customers with the equally difficult promises made to employees with the even more difficult promises made to spouse or children. Good leadership, like good poetry, is a way of holding an authentic public and private conversation at one and the same time. Where the two meet is where the leader lives and learns. At this level of understanding it demands, as one contributor to this volume writes, quoting a Zen master: "Great faith, great doubt, great effort"; it therefore demands self-knowledge. The writing of poetry has historically been the very frontier at which poets learn about themselves and their world simultaneously. This frontier is relational, conversational, and ecological. The difficult dynamic for most emerging leaders, especially male leaders in the postmodern world of work, is the movement away from command-and-control toward a far more relational and conversational way of participating—a participation that demands not only the self-belief that allows leaders to speak up but the vulnerabilities that enable them to listen.

Poetry is the art of speaking and listening at one and the same time. It is an art form that can illustrate clear and important milestones on the path to creating the more relational and conversational identity that is necessary for our future. Good poetry refuses to be read quickly or to be bent toward a too-specific meaning. Good poetry demands an entry into the timeless and untrammeled in order to comprehend it and therefore is incorruptible by the time-bound worlds on which we bring it to bear. Good poetry offers the possibility of a human identity that can be at home in a complex world without having to overwhelm or destroy it in the process. It also—and very happily—asks us to drink from pleasurable streams that nourish the core human being who is living at the center of all the work and responsibility that leadership entails. As Robert Frost declares in "Two Tramps in Mud Time":

> Only where love and need are one,
> And the work is play for mortal stakes,
> Is the deed ever really done
> For Heaven and the future's sakes.

Leading from Within is a collection of poets and poetry, illuminated so well by the comments of those whose sense of leadership has been sustained by both the writers and what they have so courageously written that we might take the liberty of quoting Frost again from his poem, "Directive":

> Here are your waters and your watering place.
> Drink and be whole again beyond confusion.

Note

"Directive" and "Two Tramps in Mud Time": From *The Poetry of Robert Frost: The Collected Poems, Complete and Unabridged*. Edited by Edward Connery Lathem. Copyright © 1969, Henry Holt and Company. Reprinted with permission of Henry Holt & Company, LLC.

Gratitudes

nobel Prize–winning poet Wislawa Szymorska tells us to seize the "extraordinary chance to follow a spark on the wind with your eyes." For the last two years, we have been blessed to spend our time amidst a veritable swirl of sparks on the wind. The sparks we are talking about are the hundreds of submissions we have received from leaders for this book.

We wish we could have assembled a seven-volume collection of poems and commentaries, because we received so many poignant contributions. In the end, the constraints of space limited us to ninety-three remarkable pieces. There are many ways to describe the diversity of this group, but perhaps most salient to a project so dependent upon e-mail is to say that we received submissions from every e-mail suffix known: .com, .edu, .gov, .org, and .net.

The commentaries not only reflect an individual's reading of a poem but a candid and brave rendering of what it means to be a leader. Taken as a collective, these men and women teach us about courage and strength, resolve and passion. One cannot be in the presence of these "sparks" without being inspired by these leaders—one and all—who are devoted to the idea that we can be something better than we are and that the release of human possibility is our collective calling.

As parents who sometimes look out into the chaos and uncertainty of our world with fear and anxiety and ask—"What will be?"—assembling this book has been an antidote to those occasional feelings of dread. We feel fortunate to have come into relationship with the underlying strength and feisty hopefulness of the leaders in this book.

Like all things worth doing, this project is entwined in a beautiful web of collaboration that suggests Walt Whitman's great poem, "A Noiseless Patient Spider." This poem, which celebrates the communal web of our lives, describes a spider building its web: "It launch'd forth filament, filament, filament, out of itself/Ever unreeling them—ever tirelessly speeding them."

In the spirit of work quilted filament by filament—thank you to so many. Sheryl Fullerton, our incomparable editor from Jossey-Bass, knew when to string the net wider and when to patch. Rick Jackson, Center for Courage & Renewal, is the maestro of tending relationships filament by filament. He worked unceasingly to secure the funding for this project and to keep us on track. Parker J. Palmer's leadership has been a beacon for this work, and his friendship and humor have been a true gift. We would also like to thank Marcy Jackson and Sharon Palmer for crucial contributions, particularly during those moments when big and ambitious projects needed wisdom and integrity.

We are grateful for the web behind the web. This includes the Lilly Endowment, Inc., and the W. K. Kellogg Foundation, which boldly and generously provided funding that supported the writing and editing of this book. Behind every institution there are people of vision and heart, and we'd like to thank Craig Dykstra, senior vice president, religion, and John Wimmer, program director, religion at Lilly, as well as Sterling K. Speirn, CEO and president, and Richard M. Foster, vice president for programs at Kellogg, for believing the world needed this book. Sam is a Group 14 Kellogg National Leadership Fellow, and we are grateful to Martha Lee and the Kellogg Fellows Leadership Alliance for getting the word out to its international network of leaders.

Megan and Sam feel a special sense of commitment to this book, knowing that all the royalties received will be used to create opportunities for leaders to participate in retreats developed by the Center for Courage & Renewal—an organization doing cutting-edge work supporting the idea that leadership must be animated from the inside out.

Our thanks to the Jossey-Bass team, especially to Joanne Clapp Fullagar, Sheri Gilbert, Sandy Siegel, Joanne Farness, and Andrea Flint.

In our intergalactic search for leaders of integrity who might be intrigued to participate in the project, we relied on a great many people to "spread the invitation." Special thanks go to Jane Bachman, Jessica Landman, Laura Rittenhouse, Doug Tanner, and Diana Chapman Walsh.

Megan writes: Every day I find myself with people who gladly give of their time and energy to make the world a better place. These tenacious and unsung leaders, too numerous to mention by name, give me hope and inspiration—thank you all. Thanks also to my parents, Ginny and Scrib, my sister Karen and brother Kevin, who each in their own way model what thoughtful leadership is all about. And special thanks to my daughters, Anya and Maya, whose insights and imagination continually open my eyes and whose laughter and love brighten each and every day, and my husband, Bruce, whose friendship, love, and support make all the difference.

Sam writes: Across my life, I have had the privilege to witness and learn from a lineup of remarkable leaders whose contributions to others evoke the heart of leadership. Thank you for modeling what it means to live with passion and work with integrity: Rob Bernheim, Ted and Tom Coghlin, Mike Copland, Dave Cotton, Elliot Eisner, Val Gardner, Rick Jackson, Rob Kunzman, Ken Miller, Elizabeth Neale, Christine O'Donnell, Joel Radmin, and Don Siegel. To my parents, Anna and Neil, and my brother Mike and sister Margo—thank you. Jake, your passion for words and ideas inspires. Kaleigh, you live in the place between imagination and the real world. That is the place of poetry. Casey, your deliberations on the ethical prefigure something important. Riley, you keep us all laughing, and what is more important than that? Lastly, to Jo: your strength and love make us all better.

CENTER FOR

Courage
& Renewal

RECONNECTING WHO YOU ARE WITH WHAT YOU DO

When we reconnect who we are with what we do, we approach our lives and our work with renewed passion, commitment, and integrity.

Since 1997, the Center for Courage & Renewal has supported teachers and leaders by fostering personal and professional renewal, through retreats that offer the time and space to reflect on life and work. These retreats—Courage to Teach and Courage to Lead—are led by skilled facilitators from diverse professions and make use of poetry and stories, solitude, reflection, and deep listening.

Developed with Parker J. Palmer and the Fetzer Institute, this approach was initially created to renew and sustain educators. Retreats are also offered to leaders in the serving professions of health care, ministry, law, and community leadership, as well as to those yearning to become more wholehearted in their life and their work.

Royalties from *Leading from Within* support the Center for Courage & Renewal's programs for leaders in a range of serving professions.

Please visit our Web site to learn more about current programs and retreats: www.CourageRenewal.org

The Editors

Sam M. Intrator, who has a Ph.D. from Stanford University, teaches at Smith College where he founded the Smith College Urban Education Initiative—an educational outreach program that places college students in internships that allow them to learn about the issues of practice and policy involving urban school reform.

Intrator has written or edited five books, including *Tuned in and Fired Up: How Teaching Can Inspire Real Learning in the Classroom* (Yale University Press, 2003), which was a finalist for the prestigious Grawemeyer Award in Education. Intrator has received a number of awards for his teaching and public service, including a Kellogg National Leadership Fellowship, an Ella Baker Fellowship, the Distinguished Teacher Award from the White House Commission of Presidential Scholars, and the Sherrerd Teaching Award.

His latest effort is the codevelopment of Project Coach—an after-school program that seeks to develop youth leadership potential in underserved communities by preparing teenagers to organize and coach sports leagues in their own neighborhoods.

Megan Scribner is an editor, researcher, and evaluator who has documented and evaluated projects for nonprofits for the past twenty-six years. She is coeditor with Sam M. Intrator of *Teaching with Fire: Poetry That Sustains the Courage to Teach* (Jossey-Bass, 2003) and editor of *Navigating the Terrain of Childhood: A Guidebook for Meaningful Parenting and Heartfelt Discipline* (Nova

Institute Press, 2004). She is coauthor, with Parker J. Palmer, of *The Courage to Teach Guide for Reflection and Renewal, Tenth Anniversary Edition* (Jossey-Bass, 2007). She has edited discussion guides, such as the one published by the World Resource Institute to accompany the Bill Moyers Reports: Earth on Edge video. She also coedited *Transformations of Myth Through Time: An Anthology of Readings* (Harcourt Brace Jovanovich, Inc., 1990); the *Joseph Campbell Transformations of Myth Through Time Study Guide;* and coauthored the project's *Faculty and Administrator's Manual.*

Scribner is an adviser to the Fetzer Institute and, with Sam M. Intrator, has evaluated a number of renewal and leadership programs. She has also taken on various leadership roles in her children's schools through the PTA and in her community as an organizer and facilitator of environmental and community issues.